KIWI MAGIC

KIWI MAGIC

ANDREW NICHOLSON
with KATE GREEN

DAVID & CHARLES

Page 2: Andrew and New York making it all look so easy at
Le Lion d'Angers

Page 6: The famous partnership: Andrew leads Spinning
Rhombus up at the World Equestrian Games, Stockholm 1990

Pages 8–9: Andrew checks his watch as he and Cartoon II fly
past the magnificent backdrop of Burghley House in 1996

Colour diagrams by Jim Bamber
All photographs by Kit Houghton except: pages 8–9,
18, 24–5, 28 and 109 by Trevor Meeks for *Horse &
Hound/Eventing*; page 23 Hugo Czerny; pages 30 and
31 by Barbara Thomson; pages 55 and 158 by Sue
Williams-Gardner (courtesy of Debbie Sly); and page
11, 12, 13, 15 and 135 by the Nicholson family

A DAVID & CHARLES BOOK

A catalogue record for this book is available from the
British Library.

ISBN 0 7153 0642 1

Book design by Visual Image
Printed in France by Imprimerie Pollina S.A.
for David & Charles
Brunel House   Newton Abbot   Devon

Contents

Foreword *by Mark Todd*

When I first knew Andrew, as a young lad in New Zealand, he already had the reputation for being a tough and talented rider who would ride any horse and get the best out of them. He was also involved in breaking in, riding racehorses and showjumping, all of which has given him a tremendous depth of knowledge.

The Nicholsons are a family who always got on and did things for themselves, so it was no surprise that fairly soon after Andrew arrived in England he found a team of horses to ride. In those early days, some of these were horses that no one else wanted to ride but, as always, he made the most of them and started getting results.

Andrew very soon made a name for himself as a fearless cross-country rider and this is part of what has made him one of the most respected three-day event riders in the world today. Coupled with an iron will, he has tremendous strength, natural balance, a good eye and a great understanding of horses, which is what makes them want to go for him.

Andrew and I have been on many teams together and because of his aptitude for cross-country riding he has often been our trailblazer. Many of New Zealand's successes are in no small way due to the advice he has given me and others on the best way to jump the fences and achieve the optimum time.

Andrew has inexhaustible energy, and since his marriage to Jayne they have built up the busiest eventing yard in the country. While Andrew loves to ride, he could not cope without Jayne, who keeps everything up to the mark for him behind the scenes. Winning consistently at all levels has been Andrew and Jayne's reward for a combination of talent and sheer hard work.

MARK TODD
*Double Olympic Champion, Open European Champion
and three-times winner of Badminton and Burghley*

HOW IT ALL BEGAN

It is often said that the reason New Zealand riders have been so successful in international eventing is that if they had the drive and determination to get themselves and their horses to the other side of the world then they were more than halfway to success already.

It is generally accepted that the strongest and best competition is in Britain, and that a rider who proves himself there has the best chance of getting on his nation's international teams. Gone are the days when the New Zealand team was a somewhat scratch affair and tended to include anyone who had a horse which had completed a clear round recently and was sound into the bargain. The rise of New Zealand as an all-conquering force in the sport has been a phenomenon of the 1990s; they currently dominate the world rankings in the sport and enjoy a devoted following in Britain.

The neighbouring Australians have been competing at top level in eventing since a group sailed to Britain in 1960 and took Badminton and the Rome Olympics by storm, but New Zealand didn't produce an Olympic team until 1984.

It all began in 1978 when a lone New Zealander, Mark Todd, contested the Lexington World Championships in the USA. His exploits, and those of such luminaries as America's Bruce Davidson, who won it, Britain's Richard Meade and the then Lucinda Prior-Palmer, were avidly watched on video in New Zealand by a fascinated seventeen-year-old Andrew Nicholson, and were to be the catalyst in his move to Britain eighteen months later.

Andrew was born in 1961 at Kihikihi, near Te Awamutu in North Island, the third of six children. His father, a dairy farmer, and his mother, a teacher, did not ride competitively, but like most country children, they were both brought up to ride and, indeed, it was their means of getting to school. Their children

Above: Andrew with his mother, Heather, winning the beautiful baby contest at Kihikihi

Right: The six Nicholson children: Andrew, aged eight, with his two brothers, John and Jamie, and three sisters, Helen, Elizabeth and Sarah

Below: Andrew and his pet calf, Cathy

Andrew and his sister Helen on their way to school on Rose and Flicker

followed a similar tradition – for a while the four eldest shared one pony, sometimes all squeezing onto the unfortunate animal together – and they weren't allowed saddles, which was probably to Andrew's advantage in later years. They lived next door to the Kihikihi showground, where there was always something going on in the way of Pony Club competitions, polo, or a large agricultural show, while the highlight of the week was bareback pony racing against the large population of local Maori children.

At the age of seven Andrew was given a pony of his own, Rajah, a 'horrible little skewbald number', who bucked whenever he was asked to canter. He would either refuse to jump or else he would buck when he got to the other side, and the partnership never remained intact for long. In the first of many deals, Rajah was swapped and given to a Maori boy who fancied the idea of riding a pinto pony, for Rose, a somewhat steadier model. Andrew and Rose attended Pony Club rallies and went hunting, which meant jumping over timber, wire and hedges without let-up for a couple of hours. However, the only prizes they won were for bareback riding and pony hurdle racing; anything remotely resembling dressage was a complete turn-off, and the young Nicholson was usually seen beating a hasty retreat from pony club when there was a dressage lesson in sight.

A teenage – and long-haired! – Andrew showjumping: 'It looks as if I've forgotten to shorten my stirrups after dressage!'

Rose was followed by dozens of other ponies who had to do everything from showing and showjumping to apple-bobbing. It was customary for New Zealand children to work their way through an entire show programme, and that included such events as 'Round the Ring', a lethal competition which involved galloping flat out with missed strides over a row of leaning five-bar gates, and another terrifying game which involved jumping backwards and forwards over a wire fence.

Andrew left school without too many regrets at the age of fifteen and joined his eldest brother John in buying young racehorses, re-schooling them and selling them. He worked for local racehorse trainers, and the daily programme was usually to ride up to twenty newly-broken horses each morning for about three trainers and then go home and ride his own. Eventing didn't play a huge part – he mostly showjumped – but he did get two horses to the country's main three-day event, which was then Sherwood, near Hawkes Bay, finishing sixth and seventh.

One of John's regular customers was Derek Kent, an English racehorse trainer, and it was he who first suggested that if Andrew really wanted to make it in eventing he should come over to England with the next shipment

Jayne, aged twenty, riding Just In Space, one of many horses she produced as a Young Rider: 'Sometimes I think Andrew only married me because I was good at flatwork!'

" Andrew has got a great ability for being able to just sit on a horse and get the best out of it, as a result of what he instinctively feels when he is going towards the first fence on it. "

Andrew Hoy,
Australian Olympic gold
medallist

of horses and ride out for him while he got himself started. The wet, sleety English January of 1980 was something of a nasty shock for the nineteen-year-old Nicholson, and he is still deeply grateful to the showjumping Powell family, with whom he went to live, especially Mrs Powell who took it upon herself to make sure the unsophisticated youngster was in the right place at the right time and wearing the right clothes.

Andrew's first introduction to the British eventing scene was grooming for Mark Todd at Badminton, despite a complete inability to plait a horse and no knowledge whatsoever of how a really big three-day event worked. As Mark actually won the event, Andrew naively assumed that it wasn't a terribly difficult sport! Badminton, with its huge crowds, was a completely alien experience after New Zealand, and he thought that obviously every British event must be like this! Andrew's first novice event, on a horse he had brought over from New Zealand to sell, was attended by the proverbial man and a dog and seemed something of a comedown!

Andrew's future in England was assured when the late Jenny Fountain, a stalwart horse trials supporter in the south, asked him to ride for her. By this stage he had met a young British rider called Jayne St John Honey, who made a strong recommendation to Jenny on Andrew's behalf and who also suggested that he might rent Jenny's half-empty yard – all of which was entirely motivated by panic that he was about to disappear back to New Zealand!

Andrew at his first Olympics, Los Angeles 1984, riding Kahlua, who was sold immediately afterwards

Happily Jayne's ploy worked and Andrew stayed with Jenny Fountain, producing event horses and persevering up the grades.

By 1984 he had two Badminton horses, Kahlua and Rubin. It was Olympic year and Andrew was told by the New Zealand selectors that all he had to do to get to Los Angeles was to produce a clear round at his first Badminton. Rubin wrote himself out of history with a cricket score of penalties, but Kahlua, who was a good cross-country performer, jumped clear and within the time to lie ninth after the second phase. He wasn't quite such a talented showjumper, and seven fences down saw the pair sink to 22nd; but it didn't matter – their Olympic ticket was assured.

Mark Todd, was, of course, the main New Zealand interest; the other team members were there, as Andrew puts it, 'just for the beer'. Mark duly won the individual gold medal, but the team wasn't disgraced, finishing sixth. Andrew and Kahlua were clear across country, but again the showjumping phase was less than glorious and this time they had five fences down. However, Andrew managed to sell Kahlua, which was part of the aim. Two American girls fell in love with Kahlua's 'cute pink nose and long eyelashes' and for the next few years he was competed successfully in the States.

Marriage to Jayne in a hasty ceremony in Mrs Nicholson Senior's garden completed a momentous year, and the pair embarked on a few years of hectic nomadic life, renting a series of yards and accumulating more and more horses. At one stage they were based with Charlotte Steel in Oxfordshire with horses lodged all around the village, and it was taking longer to walk round feeding them and mucking out than it was to ride them. However, it was thanks to Charlotte that Andrew met the horse who was to have such a major impact on his career. Charlotte was temporarily unable to compete and one of her owners, Rosemary Barlow, needed a rider for her obstreperous hunter, Spinning Rhombus. 'Piggy', as he was nicknamed because of a rather small eye, was an unprepossessing sight in those days: he was small, fat, very naughty and had an annoying habit of climbing out of his stable. Out hunting one day he reared up and removed a woman's hairnet with his front legs.

Reasoning that Piggy's naughtiness was due to boredom, Andrew decided that some novice eventing might be the answer. No one was very hopeful and Rosemary didn't even bother to go and watch, so it was with some scepticism that she received the news that her hunter had finished second on his first two outings. She sent a friend to spy on the third occasion, and they were able to report back that he had finished second yet again – and so Piggy's fate for the next five years was sealed. He started to chug his way up the grades. He wasn't the world's greatest mover, but he had a genuinely strong 'engine', coupled with plenty of stamina, courage and a placid approach. He and Andrew were often picked as trailblazers at three-day events because he had the reputation of going clear without any fuss and therefore giving confidence to the rest of the field.

By 1990 Andrew had three possible horses for the World Championships in Stockholm: the consistent Applause, known as the 'diesel horse' because his one-day event winnings had paid so

The wedding ceremony in Andrew's mother's garden in New Zealand in 1984. 'We managed to fit it in somewhere between the vet's visit and selling a horse!'

Top: Andrew winning his first three-day event, Punchestown, in 1990, on Spinning Rhombus

Above: The New Zealand team's lap of honour at the Stockholm World Games later that year

many household bills, Schiroubles and Piggy. Then Applause was ruled out after a crashing fall at the Saumur three-day event in France, and Schiroubles produced an appalling dressage test and a disastrous cross-country at Badminton; so it was all down to Piggy, who was entered for Punchestown in Ireland to see how he went. The cross-country course there was causing plenty of drama but Andrew was blissfully unaware of this. Piggy set off merrily, scrambling through the water fence which had caused so much trouble, and trundled around within the time. It was good enough to win them the competition, Andrew's first three-day event victory, and to earn them a team place for Stockholm.

Competition for the New Zealand team had increased dramatically. Mark Todd was again the figurehead, this time riding an ex-Nicholson horse, Bahlua; Blyth Tait had been in England for a year and had come second at Badminton on Messiah; and Andrew Scott had come over with a powerful black horse called Umptee. Vaughn Jefferis and Vicky Latta had also crossed the world to compete in Britain, and they rode as individuals. These six riders were to provide the first of many convincing New Zealand sweeps. Not only did they convincingly win the team gold medal, but Blyth took the individual title. Andrew, who was lying second, lost his own medal in the showjumping phase and dropped to fourth place with three fences down. Mark Todd was fifth and Andrew Scott 14th, while Vicky Latta and Vaughn Jefferis both jumped clear cross-country rounds to finish 11th and 22nd.

Andrew returned home to round off the season with second place at the inaugural Blenheim three-day event on Applause, and he also headed Britain's national points table for the first time.

By this stage Andrew and Jayne were thankfully settled in their own home with two small daughters, Melissa and Rebecca. They had bought Pleasant Spot Farm in the village of Charlton Adam, near Yeovil in Somerset, and were busily adding boxes to house the increasing number of horses, both those bought by them to sell on and those acquired from an ever-increasing band of enthusiastic and loyal owners. Jayne, who must take the credit for many of the yard's successes – she brought on Bahlua, Applause and Socrates, a horse who later represented Canada at world level – gave up competing after the arrival of Melissa complicated the Nicholsons' already complicated schedule. Often the unfortunate baby would be handed over to the cross-country starter while both her parents were out on the course, and they would return to find her screaming furiously.

In 1992 Andrew and Piggy were assured a place on the New Zealand team at the Barcelona Olympics. They put up a fantastic cross-country performance, leading for most of the day until the eventual champions Matt Ryan and Kibah Tic Toc overtook at the end. What happened next day, however, has been recorded in the annals of the sport under the heading of great disasters. New Zealand was in the lead, and Andrew entered the showjumping arena with what should have been an extremely comfortable eight-fence margin. Sadly, Piggy, with a nonchalant disregard for the importance of the moment, had already been kicking out the practice fences, and Andrew went

Andrew, Jayne, Rebecca and Melissa on a rare family 'holiday' in New Zealand

into the arena with a sinking, negative feeling about the next couple of minutes. His instinct proved horribly correct, and somehow Piggy managed to knock down *nine* fences, not only losing his own individual silver medal but demoting the team result from gold to silver. Rosemary Barlow, who was later to describe the experience as 'the worst in her life – and it was in front of the whole world', had locked herself in a portaloo with her fingers over her ears; she knew by the silence that Piggy had either gone incredibly well or incredibly badly, and as soon as she saw Andrew's thunderous expression she knew exactly which one it was.

Andrew and Jayne with Piggy's owners Mark and Rosemary Barlow, and the Piggy mascot – who still exists – after a clear show jumping and third place at Burghley

Andrew on Spinning Rhombus – minus both reins and stirrups!
– on their way to team silver at the Barcelona Olympics, 1992

Andrew on Spinning Rhombus – minus both reins and stirrups!
– on their way to team silver at the Barcelona Olympics, 1992

Barcelona was an expensive lesson but a useful one. Piggy had given notice of his showjumping weakness many times before, and in fact the best remedy was not to practise with him but to take him straight into the arena, because the length of a showjumping course was about consistent with his boredom threshold. However, a member of an Olympic team can hardly refuse to warm up his horse or to listen to training advice. Andrew later gave up jumping practice fences with Piggy and the following year he had only one rail down at Badminton. Moreover, in the autumn they finished third at Burghley with a double clear, which was a major triumph; the audience, which had been amazingly quiet and sympathetic during Piggy's round, erupted in joyous cheers when he cleared the last fence, such had the infamous Barcelona incident captured the eventing public's imagination.

*"*Andrew must be the ultimate in stickability and balance; a horse can do anything underneath him and he doesn't move. *"*

Karen Dixon,
British Olympic rider

Alternative transport in a charity race at Ston Easton. 'One of the few occasions I beat Mary King!'

New Zealand were strong favourites for the 1994 World Championships, held in The Hague in Holland, after a Kiwi-dominated Badminton: which was won by Mark Todd on a chance ride, Horton Point, with Blyth Tait second on the mare Delta, and Vaughn Jefferis, returning to England with another horse, Bounce, third; Mark was also fifth on Just An Ace. Andrew was asked to complete the team, this time riding Libby Sellars's part-Trakehner Jagermeister; the horse was only eight but had showed great jumping ability and had been placed in some three-day events on the Continent.

Sport of any kind is full of highs and lows, and the expression that 'horses are great levellers' is a tired one – but even so, there was some disbelief when three out of four New Zealanders came to grief on the cross-country: Andrew, the trailblazer, fell at the influential water complex; Blyth Tait's mare Delta had reacted badly to the shock heatwave Holland was experiencing and he retired her after a fall early on the course; while Mark Todd and Just An Ace had an inexplicable fall at the same spot as Andrew. So it was left to Vaughn to uphold honour and ensure that the individual gold medal at least was returned to New Zealand.

That year Andrew acquired three new advanced rides, which were to increase enormously his exposure at top level. He gained the ride on Kingscourt, a headstrong individual previously ridden by Paddy Muir, plus Cartoon and Buckley Province. The handsome Cartoon, owned by Maureen Rawson and John D. Wood estate agents, had clocked up an impressive record with Pippa Funnell, who adored him, but he was not the tidiest of jumpers and the pair had suffered a few tip-ups. Pippa agonised about giving up the ride, but she realised that the horse would be much better suited to Andrew.

Buckley Province had been produced to four-star level by Lynne Bevan, rider of Horton Point, who had been forced to give up her two Badminton rides due to a broken collarbone. Andrew was asked to ride Buckley Province at Badminton, but the foreign rider allocation was full so Graham Law took the ride. Lynne had experienced some refusing problems with Buckley Province, who was not always the bravest of horses, and his owner Lesley Bates decided that the horse needed a change and gave him to Andrew to ride.

Badminton has not always been Andrew's most successful event, and 1995 was no exception. He came unstuck at the Coffin fence with Jagermeister, shooting up the horse's neck and spinning round underneath but somehow

Opposite: Jagermeister exits the Badminton Lake with typical verve, on his way to 13th place in 1995

staying on – a memorable performance, TV footage of which will undoubtedly appear in a humorous sports disaster programme! The pair incurred twenty penalties in the process, and finished 13th; without this mistake they would have been fourth. Spinning Rhombus was the trailblazer again, but after eight minutes on the course Andrew realised that the old horse wasn't enjoying himself and decided to pull him up. Piggy never usually needed any urging, and when the same thing happened again at Punchestown a few weeks later, again at the eight-minute point, Andrew advised Rosemary to retire him. Piggy subsequently enjoyed being hunted by Ian McKie, master of the Bicester with Whaddon Chase, before becoming a schoolmaster for pupils at Millfield. In the summer of 1997 he was sadly put down, due to unsoundness, and buried at the Barlows' home.

Andrew felt that Buckley Province needed to consolidate at three-star level, so took him to Saumur in France, where he was second, and then to Luhmuhlen where he spectacularly somersaulted over the fourth fence, landing in the water. Unsurprisingly, at Burghley Andrew's hopes were higher of Cartoon, who had been second at Bramham that summer. In the event, however, Cartoon was fourth and Buckley Province who, Andrew felt, would either win or make a spectacular mess, won. There was no time to celebrate, though, because in typical Nicholson fashion Andrew was due to drive overland to Germany for Achselschwang CCI the next day with two horses.

A few weeks later the New Zealand team, fielding three relatively inexperienced horses, finished a close second to Britain at the Open European Championships, although being non-Europeans they were not entitled to silver medals. Andrew was 18th, riding a double clear on Two Timer, an achievement which resulted in the horse immediately attracting the attention of Japanese rider Taki Tscuhiya, who bought him as an Olympic prospect.

Throughout 1995 Andrew had fought a fascinating ding-dong battle with Bruce Davidson for the

> "One of the things I most admire about Andrew is his hard work. He obviously has enormous talent but he applies it to a huge variety of horses and is able to get a tune out of almost all of them."
>
> *Alan Smith, equestrian correspondent of* **The Daily Telegraph**

23

Keeping cool at the 1996 Olympics in Atlanta

> **"** Anyone wanting a lesson in riding should watch the video of Andrew coming down the Beaufort Staircase at Badminton. His horse hit the top palisade quite violently but Andrew's lower leg never moved, which is typical of him. **"**
>
> *Giles Rowsell,*
> *Windsor director and*
> *British selector*

Land Rover FEI World Rankings title, an accolade which carried much kudos among riders. The struggle for supremacy lasted right up until the very last CCI of the year, Puhinui in New Zealand, where Andrew needed to finish second to win the title, and created unprecedented media interest. Andrew was generously offered a horse for Puhinui by South Islander Olivia Waddy and flew to New Zealand four days before the event in a bid to win the World Rankings title on home ground. Publicity for the event reached an all-time high on both New Zealand and Sky television and in reams of newsprint.

When Andrew took his chance ride Tolman into second place after the cross-country, the miracle seemed possible; but in some horrendously unseasonal weather a tired Tolman hit three fences in the boggy showjumping ring, lowering Andrew to an unhelpful fourth place.

For the 1996 Olympic year, Andrew had a plethora of top-level rides: the athletic Mister Maori, the smooth-moving Dawdle, Buckley Province, Cartoon and Jagermeister. The selectors decided that Andrew should be allowed a crack at both the team and individual competitions in Atlanta, and he advised them that Jagermeister would be the more reliable team horse, while Buckley Province, who could be either brilliant or disastrous, would be better reserved for the individual effort, which carried less responsibility towards anyone else.

Ever since Atlanta was named as the Olympic venue for 1996, the three-day event had been dogged by controversy because of the unsuitability of the humid climate for horses. Although New Zealand was favourite to win, Andrew was less than inspired by the thought of spending a whole month away from home acclimatising for a competition which, in the opinion of many people, shouldn't be happening at all.

As it happened, the weather was milder than expected and conditions in the early morning of team cross-country day were positively balmy. The speed and endurance phase had been shortened and modified, and there were a number of cooling breaks for the horses. Unfortunately Jagermeister was so fit and hyped up that the compulsory cooling halts only served to fire him up more: he pulled Andrew's arms out worse than ever before, and at the water complex jumped up onto the central bank with far too much gusto, promptly landing on top of the fence off the bank – of course he was then unable to jump it, and unceremoniously stopped, almost unseating his jockey.

The rest of the team, having acquitted themselves so well in the dressage phase that they were in with a definite winning chance,

Opposite: Andrew on Buckley Province at the Atlanta Olympics

did not fare too happily either. Blyth Tait had done a masterful job as trailblazer, although the going was so slippery that he did not dare let the brakes off as much as he would have liked. Vicky Latta suffered a horrible-looking fall and was compelled to retire because her horse had a bloody nose, and Vaughn Jefferis's mount Bounce was suffering from the effects of the weather and had to be nursed around slowly. All things considered, they did well to win the bronze medal.

In the individual competition Andrew and Buckley Province were well placed after the dressage, but when travelling smoothly on the cross-country, they over-jumped into a water fence – which had been dyed a lurid azure blue at the last minute – and, to horrified gasps from supporters, crumpled on landing. However, the competition still became the Kiwis' own, with Blyth taking the individual gold medal and Sally Clark the bronze.

Back at home, a spate of high placings both on the national scene and in the autumn three-day events in Europe – which included a frustrating run of second places – saw Andrew finish at the top of the national points leaderboard for the seventh time – this time on 1,349 points and with a margin of 305 over his nearest rival Mark Todd – and third in the world rankings behind Blyth Tait and Mark.

The following year, 1997, promised much, with strength in depth in advanced horses, many of whom had become established in their flatwork and able to gain the dressage advantage which has become so crucial for success in the 1990s: but it was not a great year!

Serious over-subscription to Badminton meant that overseas riders were limited to one ride each – an unpopular ruling in the light of the fact that some British riders had two horses, and one which caused much heated discussion and forced the sport to re-assess Badminton's status on the world stage. Andrew had a choice of four horses and eventually chose Cartoon over Jagermeister, whose owners, Michael and Libby Sellars, were most understanding. It proved the wrong choice; Cartoon's ideal going is the smoothness of a bowling green and halfway around the wet, muddy Badminton course he slipped and did the splits. By some miracle, Andrew stayed on board, but it rather knocked the stuffing out of this genuine horse and a few fences later he ran out at the top of the Beaufort Steps.

At a rainsoaked Punchestown on the following weekend, Jagermeister disgraced himself by pulling so wildly that he slowed himself up and incurred too many time penalties to be in the prizes. Punchestown also saw the ending of Andrew's erratic partnership with Buckley Province who, having gone well up to that point, threw in the towel at a water complex. The pair were submerged, but the partnership came up for air intact, much to the watching crowd's

" Andrew is fearless. His confidence is such that he has no fear of the inability of any horse he rides and he instils that confidence in them. "

Robert Lemieux,
director of the International
Event Riders Association

Opposite: Andrew on Two Timer at the European Championships in 1995

Overleaf: How *did* he do that? Andrew displays his 'ultimate stickability' in this near-miss at Gatcombe on – and off! – Spinning Rhombus

HOW IT
ALL BEGAN

Max the puppy falls at
the first!

amusement, only for Buck to put in a stop. Andrew decided to return the horse to his owners, feeling that he could not do him justice at top level any more.

There was some light relief in the performances of the younger horses at two and three-star level and Jagermeister redeemed himself with a calmer performance, thanks to a new sweet-iron gag bit, to finish second at Luhmuhlen CCI in Germany. The new CIC (international one-day event) at Chantilly in France, which carried generous prize money, was another particularly good weekend. Riding Dawdle and Cartoon, Andrew finished second and third behind Mary King and stood to be well rewarded in the new Chantilly-Gatcombe points challenge.

At Gatcombe, Cartoon obliged to finish fifth in the British Open Championships, but Dawdle, who Andrew had nominated as his points-scoring horse in the Chantilly-Gatcombe challenge and who was lying second going into the cross-country phase, produced the neurotic behaviour of which he is occasionally capable. First he refused to start, kicking out and scattering ropes, Jayne and sundry officials in his wake. He then set off erratically and, seconds later, put in a sharp run-out.

Andrew's misfortunes continued at Blair, where King Leo, lying second after the cross-country and thrilling his enthusiastic and supportive owners, Daniel and Deborah Burrell, knocked out a couple of showjumps and plummeted to eighth. Meanwhile, Sir Samuel had showed a distinct lack of enthusiasm on the cross-country and eventually ground to a halt at a covered fence, at which point the roof fell in on Andrew's head and he retired, deciding that someone was trying to tell him something!

The Blenheim weekend, which saw riders take a day off from proceedings in respect of the funeral of Diana, Princess of Wales, produced two encouraging cross-country performances from New York and Highly Rated, but the day was greatly marred by the tragic death of an Irish rider, Samuel Moore. Andrew had to go across country shortly after the accident and, news of the tragedy having filtered through to those riders delayed for an hour in the 10-minute box, it required considerable mental determination and detachment to carry on.

It was, therefore, a sombre lead up to the Burghley Open Europeans which started two days later. Andrew was selected for the team with either Cartoon or Dawdle, but once again, 'wrong horse syndrome' prevailed. His preferred ride Cartoon is not the smartest of movers at a trot-up, and when the ground jury asked for a second look at him at the first horse inspection, the New Zealand selectors became unnerved and insisted Andrew ride

Dawdle instead as team trailblazer. The pair produced New Zealand's second-best dressage test, but Dawdle's slightly ungenerous run-out on the cross-country put paid both to their individual medal chances and probably cost New Zealand the team gold. Dawdle finished the course well and fast, but he was slightly jarred and next day it was decided not to showjump him, but to save him for another day.

A trip to Achselschwang in Germany, a favourite event, provided some compensation when Andrew finished third on Cartoon. Mary King won the competition, which led Andrew to comment that following Mary and her first prize of an Audi around the arena on a mountain bike, which was his prize, rather summed up the 1997 season! Andrew also won a weekend trip to Venice but, needless to say, it remained to be seen whether he and Jayne would find the time!

Boekelo CCI in Holland was another disaster. Andrew was only allowed to ride one horse and he optimistically reasoned that this would give him more chance to concentrate on one horse, Merillion, and that this would be successful. They had a brilliant cross-country round in the wet conditions, the second fastest of the day, but next day Merillion was found to be unsound at the final trot-up and was ignominiously spun. Another long drive home.

The final indignity came at Le Lion d'Angers when, having been delighted with the young Star Role's performance and pleasantly surprised by the newly-learned galloping prowess of Valhalla, a young horse who Andrew didn't think would make the grade, he found himself sitting on the floor in the showjumping arena amid a sea of poles. Valhalla, a careful horse, was lying fourth and in a possible winning position, but he 'put down' before a fence, shooting Andrew out of the front door and causing surprised gasps from a large French crowd, who expecting anything but that to happen.

Thus ended a less-than-vintage year — but all riders have them. Andrew's results were still good enough, though, to make him the national points leader for a record eighth successive year and also place him fifth in the Land Rover FEI World Rankings and in the winning New Zealand team.

The Nicholsons' yard is currently full to bursting – more horses keep arriving from new owners – and Jayne works even harder to keep the whole operation running smoothly. New Zealand's 'old firm' of Andrew, Mark, Blyth and Vaughn are still very much at the head of affairs in the sport, although Vicky Latta has retired from competition, but new younger riders are beginning to track their footsteps and the New Zealand federation is beginning to realise that they cannot rely on their talents for ever. However, Andrew has no intention of giving up while the bringing-on of young horses and the thrill of riding them across country proves so strong.

" Why is Andrew Nicholson a great cross-country rider? Because he can't do dressage and showjumping! No, seriously, his strength is his consistency – he's an out-and-out performer who always produces the goods and his results speak for themselves. He can also stay on! You can count on one hand the times he's fallen off. "

Blyth Tait, team-mate and Olympic champion

Overleaf: Andrew on his magnificent winning round at Burghley riding Buckley Province in 1995

CAREER HIGHLIGHTS

1990 1st Punchestown (Spinning Rhombus)
4th and team gold Stockholm World Equestrian Games (Spinning Rhombus)
2nd Blenheim (Applause)

1991 6th and 15th Burghley (Applause and Spinning Rhombus)
1st Blenheim (Park Grove)
6th Le Lion d'Angers (Jumbo)

1992 2nd Windsor (Pilot Light)
16th and team silver Barcelona Olympic Games (Spinning Rhombus)
16th Boekelo (Spinning Rhombus)
1st Pau (Optimist I)
7th Le Lion d'Angers (Gumley)

1993 1st British Intermediate Championships (Jagermeister)
6th Chantilly (Olympic Star)
2nd Luhmuhlen (Optimist I)
12th Badminton (Spinning Rhombus)
3rd and 11th Burghley (Spinning Rhombus and Optimist I)
3rd Waregem (Walk On Cloud)
4th Pau (Fine Time II)
4th Le Lion d'Angers (Jagermeister)
2nd Land Rover FEI World Rankings

1994 6th Punchestown (Celebrity)
18th Saumur (Jagermeister)
3rd Bramham (Walk On Cloud)
13th Chantilly (Cabalva April Fool)
4th Compiègne (Fine Time II)
Completed World Games, team sixth place (Jagermeister)
15th Blair Castle (Walk On Top)
2nd British Intermediate Championships (Walk On Top)
7th Burghley (Spinning Rhombus)
7th and 9th Boekelo (Jagermeister and Olympic Star)
1st Achselschwang (Buckley Province)
6th Pau (Fine Time II)

1995 2nd and 7th Saumur (Buckley Province and Olympic Star)
13th Badminton (Jagermeister)

2nd Bramham (Cartoon)
2nd Compiègne (Dawdle)
1st and 4th Burghley (Buckley Province and Cartoon)
2nd and 5th Achselschwang (Mister Maori and Celebrity)
15th and second-placed team Open European Championships (Two Timer)
4th Puhinui (Tolman)
2nd Land Rover FEI World Rankings

1996 7th Saumur (Mister Maori)
7th and 12th Badminton (Buckley Province and Cartoon)
3rd Luhmuhlen (Jagermeister)
Team bronze Olympics (Jagermeister)
3rd British Open Championships (Dawdle)
2nd Burghley (Cartoon)
2nd Blenheim (Dawdle)
4th Blair Castle (New York)
2nd and 7th Achselschwang (Star Role and Majestic Style)
9th Boekelo (Jagermeister)
3rd Land Rover FEI World Rankings
1st National Leaderboard

1997 3rd Saumur (Dawdle)
8th and 14th Compiègne (Highly Rated and Star Role)
Completed Badminton (Cartoon)
8th Windsor (Whit Monday)
4th Breda (Just Zulu)
2nd and 3rd Chantilly (Dawdle and Cartoon)
2nd Luhmuhlen (Jagermeister)
5th British Open at Gatcombe (Cartoon II)
8th Blair Castle (King Leo)
10th Blenheim (Highly Rated)
Member of silver-medal winning NZ team at Burghley Open Europeans (Dawdle)
3rd Achselschwang (Cartoon II)
4th Le Lion d'Angers (Star Role)

5th in Land Rover FEI World Rankings
1st in National BHTA rankings for the 8th successive time

WHAT I LOOK FOR IN A HORSE

Pleasant Spot Farm is probably the busiest eventing yard in the country, with an average total of twenty-seven inmates. Of those, between ten and fifteen horses actually belong to Andrew – and it goes without saying that they are all for sale, because the Nicholson yard is strictly a business. Andrew and Jayne buy a maximum of fifteen horses a year, with ex-racehorses being by far the favourite type of purchase. About half the new intake will be bought at the winter bloodstock sales, especially Doncaster in December, and they will be Thoroughbred horses aged between three and six years old, all of whom will have raced at least a couple of times. These horses tend to have a genuine reason for sale, the bottom line being that they are too slow for racing. The second very good reason for buying ex-racehorses is that they are cheap.

About four of the newcomers will arrive from New Zealand, and sometimes they are bought unseen, with Andrew relying on the judgement of his eldest brother John, who breaks in and trains racehorses, or one of the trainers he worked for in his teens, most notably Kevin Myers. Kevin produced Bahlua, who after leaving Andrew's hands became one of the most consistent three-day event horses in the world. He went on to win a gold medal at the Stockholm World Championships with Mark Todd and a European bronze medal in 1993 with Dutch rider Eddy Stibbe. Again, these New Zealand-bred horses are cheap, with prices low enough to justify paying an air fare to Britain on top of the purchase figure.

Andrew's method of acquiring horses is fairly unique in that the majority of event riders like to be able to take their time to try out a potential purchase. Obviously you can't sit on a horse at a bloodstock sale – in fact you are lucky if you see it trot. Andrew reasons that the more you try a horse over lavish facilities, the more expensive it will be

and the more you will end up looking for faults in the horse. His attitude is that endless trying of a horse will only raise your expectations of it and make you impatient if things go wrong. Andrew feels that if you don't expect too much of a horse you will start off with a better, more patient understanding of it.

Tales of Andrew flying to New Zealand for twenty-four hours to view a horse are grossly exaggerated, but it is true that he doesn't waste much time, and can't understand why anyone needs more than a day to find a new young horse! About five days is all that is allowed for the annual 'holiday' at home, during which time John Nicholson will have arranged for Andrew and Jayne to view a selection of ex-racehorses. On these occasions Andrew might actually get to ride a potential purchase, usually giving it a quick 'pop' over a few natural obstacles. As far as the Nicholsons are concerned, the ones which show the most natural athletic ability are the most economically viable prospects and will qualify for the flight home. Only rarely do the Nicholsons buy a horse with eventing form or one that is home-bred, because they will be too expensive. Economy is the deciding factor.

The rest of the horses in the yard belong to a selection of loyal owners, the majority of whom are British. This is a phenomenon that has occasionally caused disquiet on the circuit, with mutterings about the 'foreigners' pinching rides from the British. When Sue Benson dared to write in *Eventing* magazine that it was a pity more British owners couldn't be patriotic and support the home riders, the outcry from owners with horses in the yards of New Zealand, Australian and Swedish riders – to name but a few nations – was vociferous. Riders pointed out that they were paying mortgages and taxes like everyone else, some are married to English wives, and as far as the sport is concerned,

WHAT I LOOK FOR IN A HORSE

not only are they paying the same in entry fees and registrations, but their presence at an event undeniably enhances the status of that horse trial and raises the standard of competition. The Nicholsons, among other couples, have been in England for so long that, like anyone else, they have friends who want to support them. Moreover, Andrew is sometimes persuaded to take on horses which other British riders have either turned down or cannot get on with. He has also, occasionally, volunteered to swap one of his horses with another rider for a more difficult model – although he is more fussy than he was in the early 'hungry' days, and while he will always look at a horse and proffer honest, and sometimes blunt advice, he will not now necessarily take the ride.

'When I first see a horse, it has got to have something about it that makes me want to see more, and that's obviously the effect I hope it will have on a customer. I buy a lot of youngsters from sales without riding them, so the criteria then is that they must look purposeful and as if they've got "things to do". I bought Climb The Heights from Doncaster, having only seen him walk around the sale ring, and in his first season eventing he won four out of five competitions entered.

'Although breeding is the last thing I worry about if I like the type, in theory I will usually go for a horse which is full Thoroughbred. One good reason is the price – they tend to be cheaper than home-bred horses – but the other factor is that I want a horse with a relentless gallop, which is something that even slow racehorses have; if a horse hasn't got this naturally, it never will have. At least, I haven't found a way to magically transform a slow horse into a quick one!

'Many riders are put off ex-racehorses because they worry that they will be difficult to train in the showjumping and dressage phases. It is true that this can take a little longer than with a half-bred horse, but I am used to working with Thoroughbreds and I find them teachable and intelligent. When I took Turtle, a New Zealand Thoroughbred, to his

first novice event he achieved a dressage score of 28, had just one showjump down and went clear across country, having only arrived at the yard two months previously.

'I think that because a Thoroughbred is designed for galloping, it tends to last longer and stay sounder. Thoroughbreds have greater reserves of stamina, which is something that has become more important in recent years with many championships being held in hot weather. The Atlanta Olympics were obviously a case in point, but the World Championships at The Hague in Holland in 1994 caught everyone by surprise with a shock heatwave, and there have been some years when it has even been quite hot at Badminton or Burghley.

'When looking at a potential purchase, a lot of people will look at the horse's bad points first and be put off; I look for its good points and work from there. The only thing I really insist on is good limbs: a horse doesn't have to have ten inches of bone if it is only 16hh, but the bone it has must be good, with clean, flat-looking lines.

'If a horse has pleasing limbs, then I will often overlook other defects. I wouldn't be put off by a horse with a long back because this sort tends to be very scopey jumping across country, although it might find it a bit more difficult to showjump clear. I recently acquired a horse from New Zealand called Double Edge who has a long back and a short neck, but he is still a very attractive horse, a nice strong "chocolate"-chestnut colour, and he shows plenty of scope.

'Turtle has a mild roach back, which is something I don't mind, although I wouldn't buy a horse that was any worse than him because a real "roachy" back can cause problems later on and a horse could be penalised for it when being vetted for purchase. I would also forgive a horse with a bit of a ewe neck if it had other good points, although again there are limits, and I wouldn't want it if it looked like a scrawny, ugly duckling. However, a ewe neck *is* something that can be improved with training. Mister Maori is a bit ewe-necked, but he is

one of the best cross-country horses I have ridden.

'We sometimes end up with horses which have "undesirable" habits such as windsucking or weaving, but I don't consider that to be the end of the world. I'd rather have a good horse which crib-bites than a useless one with no bad habits!

'Appearance isn't everything: an important point to remember is that you can change a horse's outlook through work and, therefore, by giving him self-confidence. Spinning Rhombus looked like a fat, hairy pony when I first got him; he stood in an unprepossessing manner and I thought novice would be his limit, but he had a much bigger engine than we realised. He was nicknamed Piggy because he had a tiny eye, but somehow he always looked much more generous in action; he was a classic case of a horse who gained in confidence and started to look more impressive as he did so.

'And when Mister Maori arrived I thought he was hideous. Usually I can't wait to try a horse, but with him I went into the house and had a cup of coffee first! But after I'd sat on him for a couple of minutes he stopped putting his head on one side and felt quite smart; and he was even better over a few poles.

'Of the horses pictured here, I would expect the youngsters Mr Glitz, King Leo and Sir Samuel to look quite different in a year's time. All the others have done three-day events, which gives them a fitter, harder look; and although Turtle is only five, he has that look already because he hasn't been long out of racing.

'When looking for an event horse there is no distinct, correct pattern because they come in all manner of shapes, sizes and types. Although good conformation can ultimately play a significant part in the horse's soundness, in my opinion the most important factor is what lies between its ears. I find that the good ones are always generous and overcompensate for their conformation defects, and the bad ones ultimately depend only on their good attributes to bring them through!'

Whit Monday 9yo Thoroughbred bay gelding, 17.3hh, by Suny Boy

I would imagine that as a young horse he was probably very weak and gangly, and he has taken time to mature – he is huge!

This horse is much bigger than I would normally choose, but he is very agile and can shorten his stride as easily as he can lengthen it. He is a great mover and has good hindlegs with strong hocks, which is important because a big horse needs to have his hocks underneath him naturally. He was bred to race, and won a point-to-point as a five-year-old. Whit Monday was sent to me to start eventing in 1996; he jumps well and went advanced in his first year, finishing sixth at his first three-day event, the two-star CCI at Pau in France. He is by the same sire as Bertie Blunt, who won Badminton in 1996 with Mark Todd.

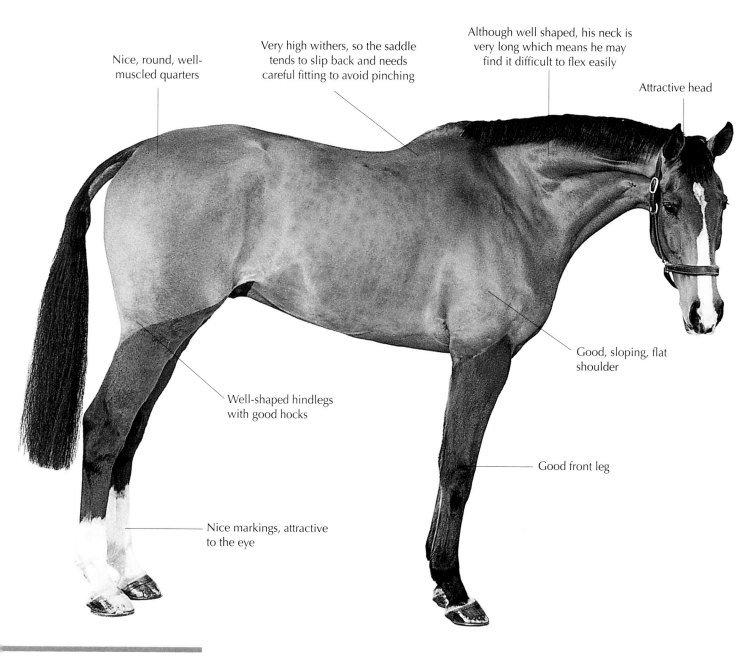

Nice, round, well-muscled quarters

Very high withers, so the saddle tends to slip back and needs careful fitting to avoid pinching

Although well shaped, his neck is very long which means he may find it difficult to flex easily

Attractive head

Well-shaped hindlegs with good hocks

Good, sloping, flat shoulder

Good front leg

Nice markings, attractive to the eye

Buckley Province 15yo Thoroughbred bay gelding, 16hh, by Twinkling Haste

Ideal type, although a little small for most people. A dinky little horse with a pretty head; he looks as if he should be sitting on a mantelpiece! Buckley Province also started life in National Hunt racing, though not very successfully. I took over the ride on him from Lynne Bevan, who had produced him to four-star level; he had developed a tendency to stop, however, and his owners decided he needed a change of scenery. Although he is a light little horse he is well put together, compact and naturally balanced. He has good conformation and front legs, being not too long in the cannon bones or pasterns. He has strong, robust limbs for his size. He is not the bravest horse – although having said that, he did win the big one at Burghley.

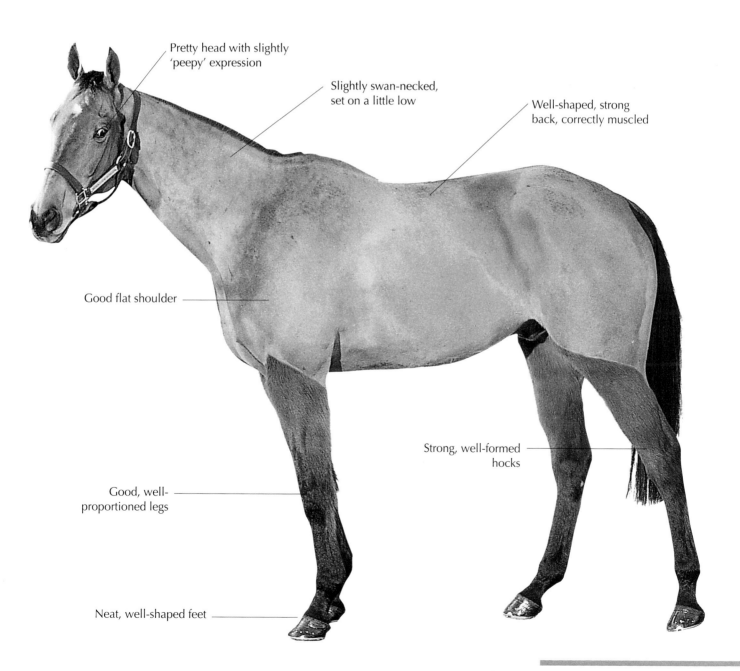

Pretty head with slightly 'peepy' expression

Slightly swan-necked, set on a little low

Well-shaped, strong back, correctly muscled

Good flat shoulder

Strong, well-formed hocks

Good, well-proportioned legs

Neat, well-shaped feet

Mister Maori 8yo New Zealand Thoroughbred chestnut gelding, 16.1hh, by Brilliant Invader

A real machine to ride across country! He is easily the best jumper in the yard. He is not an impressive horse to look at, and these photographs are a good example of how a horse's appearance can improve with the addition of tack and a rider – and when he arrived here as a four-year-old I wondered what on earth I'd got. My brother John broke him in as a two-year-old in New Zealand and described him as an 'old man', because apparently he looked like a ten-year-old even then! He was brought over to England by the former National Hunt trainer David Barons, who buys a lot of New Zealand horses, but he was too slow for racing. He is a bit ewe-necked

and doesn't 'stand under himself' naturally, but he is very athletic and a good jumper. Across country it's as if he has an inbuilt gearbox: you can set him at whatever speed you want and he will then just keep lobbing along. He's very obedient and a real gentleman.

Mister Maori was sixth at his first three-day event as a six-year-old and seventh at the Saumur CCI*** at seven. The reason he didn't show ability as a racehorse was probably because his shape was against him; he needed time to come to full strength. He might be quite impressive if he was raced now. He is by the same sire as Blyth Tait's Olympic Champion, Ready Teddy.

Slightly ewe neck, which has improved by working in a correct outline

Weak through the back, which means it has taken him longer to build up the correct muscle

Lovely noble head with a good expression

Good flat shoulder

He doesn't 'stand under himself' naturally

He is very straight in the hind leg. This means he finds collected work difficult

Stands very close behind; this can result in brushing

Nice short cannon bones

With tack and rider, Mister Maori suddenly looks much smarter. It hides his faults, gives him more presence and enhances the alert look on his face

Jagermeister II 11yo bay gelding, 16hh, by Polarschnee

This horse is an exceptional jumper, but he has an extremely strong neck and is very headstrong, and difficult to contain!

This horse's breeding is unusual for one of ours in that he is part warmblood. He was bred in New Zealand, but his sire is a German-bred Trakehner; his dam is half pony, half Thoroughbred. Nevertheless, apart from the way he stands and the shape of his neck – he reaches forwards, which is typical of a Trakehner – you could pass him off as a Thoroughbred. He is the strongest horse I have ever ridden because he wants to stretch his neck out,

rather than bringing it in; if he would just let me *ride* him a bit more on the cross-country, he would be one of the best. He's not that big, but when you sit on him he gives the impression of being a huge, powerful horse. He feels very different from Thoroughbreds in that they perform out of lightness, whereas he operates out of sheer power.

Jagermeister is New Zealand-owned by Libby Sellars; he has been placed in all his three-day event outings – apart from the 1992 World Games where I managed to fall off him – and he was my Olympic team horse last year, when he pulled my arms out.

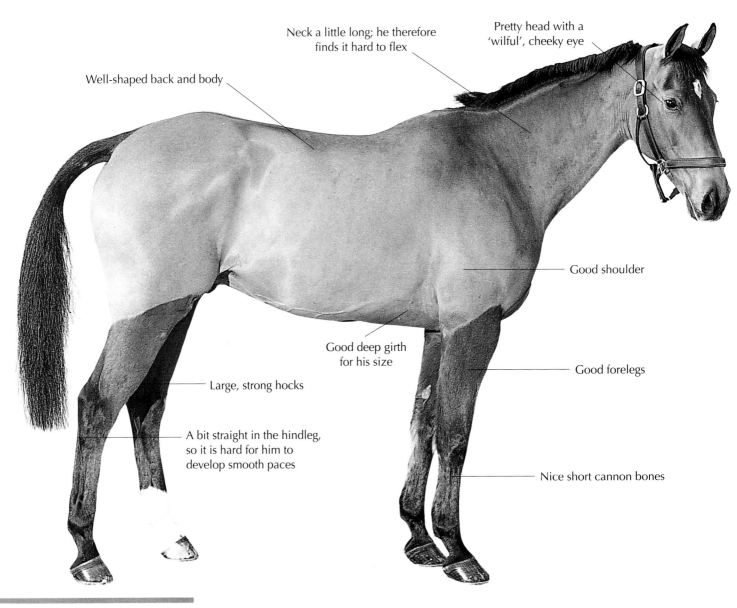

Neck a little long; he therefore finds it hard to flex

Pretty head with a 'wilful', cheeky eye

Well-shaped back and body

Good shoulder

Good deep girth for his size

Good forelegs

Large, strong hocks

A bit straight in the hindleg, so it is hard for him to develop smooth paces

Nice short cannon bones

Dawdle 9yo Thoroughbred bay gelding, 16.2hh, by Saunter

A classical masterpiece at first sight – but on closer examination, a forgery!

He is a good size and has a lovely shoulder with a well-set-on neck. If he has a fault, it is that he is weak in his hindlegs: he is a little light of bone and his hocks are not as strong for his size as those of Buckley Province or Whit Monday. But Dawdle is a lovely horse to sit on, like a Rolls Royce, with plenty of front, and he is a smooth mover at all paces. His pretty head is deceptive, though: he is actually quite a tricky character and would love to kick you. He is a highly strung horse but has masses of ability, and is one I would expect to go to the top.

Dawdle is owned by Selina Boyce; he was third in the British Open Championships at Gatcombe, second at Blenheim in 1996, and third at Saumur in 1997. His sire was a successful flat racehorse.

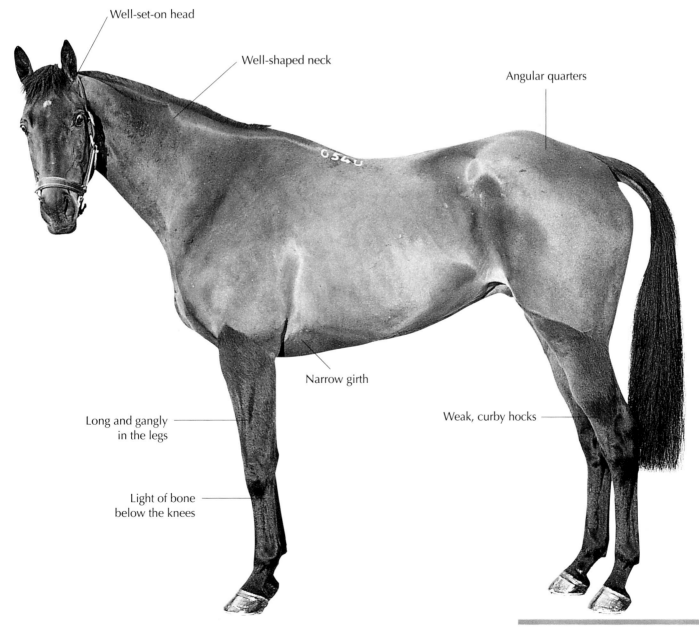

Well-set-on head

Well-shaped neck

Angular quarters

Narrow girth

Long and gangly in the legs

Weak, curby hocks

Light of bone below the knees

Mr Glitz 6yo bay gelding, 16.2hh, by Jumbo

Because of his shape this horse finds it effortless to jump, and he has lovely loose paces.

This would be many people's ideal type, and as soon as I saw Mr Glitz in the stable I wanted to try him: he had a look which said 'Come and play with me'. He is a stronger sort of horse than I would normally go for – it is the Irish Draught blood from his sire, who was an international eventer – but he is a good mover, being light on his feet, and he has a big, scopey jump. He has good conformation and strong limbs without being heavy. I broke him as a three-year-old, after which he was sent to another yard where he bucked a few people off – he can certainly get off the ground! I started eventing him as a five-year-old and he upgraded to intermediate in a year; he was then turned out for a bit. When he has done a bit more work I expect him to look more the shape of our older advanced horses, even though he is not a Thoroughbred. This horse was subsequently sold to a well-known international rider, Eddy Stibbe, who re-named him Earl Grey.

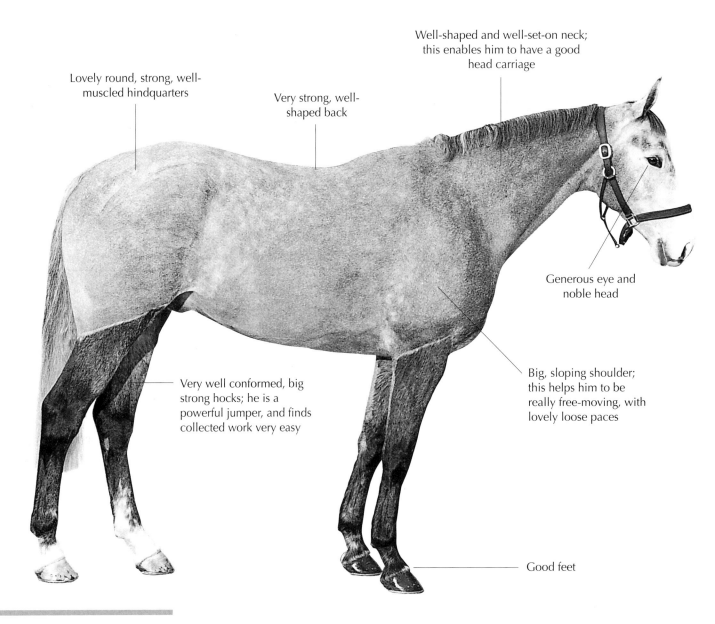

Lovely round, strong, well-muscled hindquarters

Very strong, well-shaped back

Well-shaped and well-set-on neck; this enables him to have a good head carriage

Generous eye and noble head

Very well conformed, big strong hocks; he is a powerful jumper, and finds collected work very easy

Big, sloping shoulder; this helps him to be really free-moving, with lovely loose paces

Good feet

King Leo 7yo Irish-bred grey gelding, 16.3hh, by Hildenly

He won most of his starts in 1997, despite occasional weaknesses in the showjumping.

I have a thing about a horse being able to 'fit into a square box' when you look at it. Compared to the others, King Leo looks as if he'd be better in a rectangular one! Yet he has good limbs – it's just his initial appearance that would put me off! Nevertheless under saddle he is an impressive horse. He had already been novice evented when he was sent to me by his owners Daniel and Deborah Burrell in 1997, and as long as I can improve his showjumping, I think he has enough quality to go international.

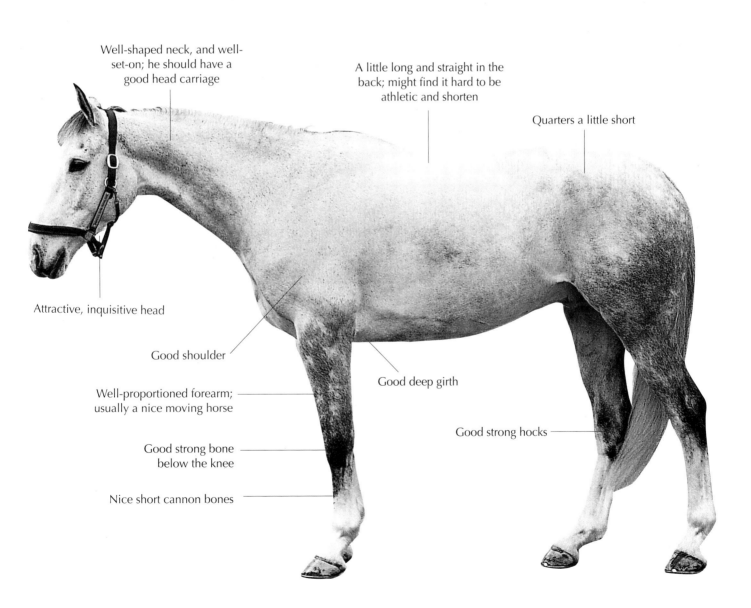

Well-shaped neck, and well-set-on; he should have a good head carriage

A little long and straight in the back; might find it hard to be athletic and shorten

Quarters a little short

Attractive, inquisitive head

Good shoulder

Good deep girth

Well-proportioned forearm; usually a nice moving horse

Good strong hocks

Good strong bone below the knee

Nice short cannon bones

Turtle 5yo New Zealand Thoroughbred bay gelding, 16hh, by Sir Sian

I expect to alter this horse's shape with correct schooling. However, even with the immature weaknesses shown here, he is a very impressive performer and should win points very easily.

Turtle only arrived in the yard six weeks before this picture was taken; I bought him unseen as a three-year-old from a flat trainer in New Zealand, and when I saw him a year later I wasn't that impressed with the way he looked. My brother ran him on the flat with a view to

training him over hurdles; he didn't run that well on the flat, but John was impressed with his jumping and suggested I evented him. I wasn't convinced – but sure enough, he *can* jump!

Turtle has a long way to go, but he is a definite candidate for the big stuff. He is not very big, but he is athletic and a serious jumper. He is well put together with a good length of neck – not too long and not too short.

Anxious, slightly nervous eye, although it should improve

Slightly ewe-necked; this will, we hope, change with correct schooling

Slight roach back

Good, strong, deep chest

Somewhat weak behind

'Stands over himself' in front

A little light of bone

Cartoon II 13yo bay gelding, 16.2hh, by Cosmos

This horse's generous nature – you could have him in your house! – and good attitude makes up for what he lacks in natural ability; he's the sort that can be 'man-made'.

His nickname is Leggy, for obvious reasons. However, even though his legs *are* a bit too long, they have kept him going so far, and he certainly has a pretty smart three-day event record, thus proving they are tough enough. Furthermore, it is far easier to have a horse which stands correctly naturally, as opposed to the way

Jagermeister stands, for example; and Cartoon has an elegant look, carrying his head well. He isn't pure Thoroughbred, having a touch of both Arab and Irish Draught, but he is built like one.

Cartoon was bred by his owner Maureen Rawson, and before she sent him to me he had built up a consistent record with Pippa Funnell. Cartoon is not renowned for his showjumping ability and his legs are a bit dangly across country, but he gets to the other side and the advantage about him is that he *lets* you ride him!

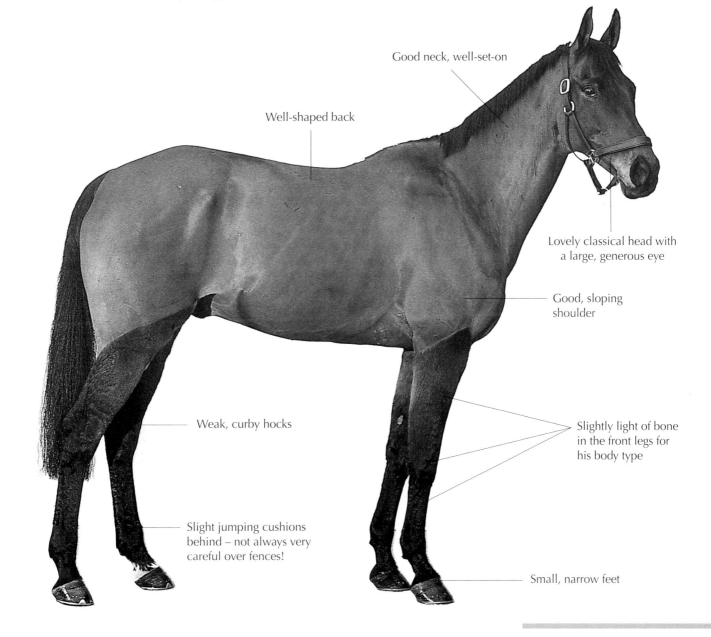

Good neck, well-set-on

Well-shaped back

Lovely classical head with a large, generous eye

Good, sloping shoulder

Weak, curby hocks

Slightly light of bone in the front legs for his body type

Slight jumping cushions behind – not always very careful over fences!

Small, narrow feet

Majestic Style 7yo New Zealand Thoroughbred bay gelding, 16.1hh, by Take Your Partner

A very good galloper and jumper, but he has slightly more knee action in his trot than is desirable.

My favourite horse: he has an athletic look, and he 'fits in the square box'. He has a nice head without looking soft – he looks uncomplicated and brave, which he is – and he has good limbs. Majestic Style had won on the flat in New Zealand but wasn't good enough to carry on racing. He was placed in his first three-day event, at Achselschwang, and is now advanced. He doesn't have the best trot for dressage – it has a little too much knee action – but it is even in rhythm, and his jumping makes up for it.

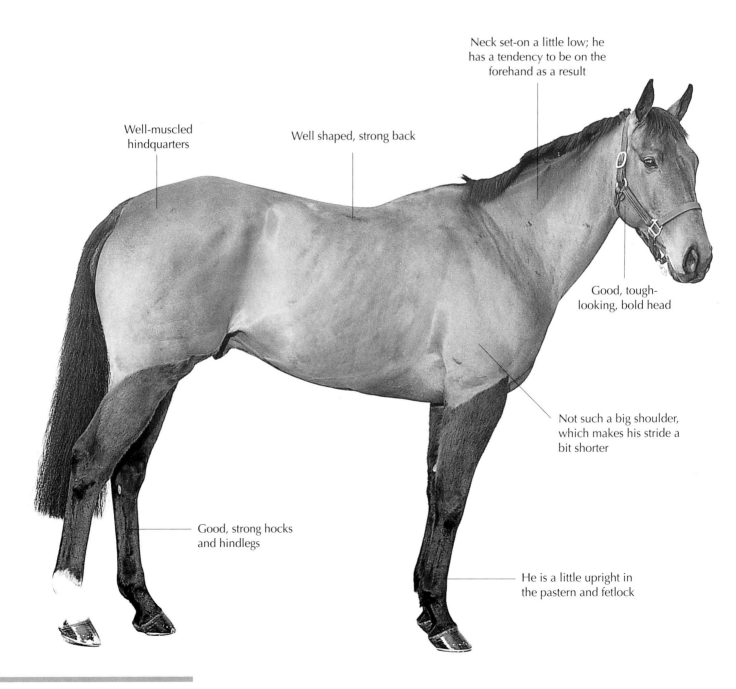

Neck set-on a little low; he has a tendency to be on the forehand as a result

Well-muscled hindquarters

Well shaped, strong back

Good, tough-looking, bold head

Not such a big shoulder, which makes his stride a bit shorter

Good, strong hocks and hindlegs

He is a little upright in the pastern and fetlock

Star Role 7yo Thoroughbred chestnut gelding, 16.1hh, by Morgan's Choice

Basically a good pattern of horse, and a very good mover and jumper; a similar type to Spinning Rhombus.

Star Role came from my neighbour, the National Hunt trainer Ron Hodges, who had run him twice over hurdles and found him too slow. Ron asked me to come over and give the horse a jump – and I have had him ever since. He is a bit low in his wither, but he is very strong, and he is level-headed, has even paces and is a careful jumper. In fact he must have been a nightmare ride for a

jockey in a hurdle race because he jumps very extravagantly, getting high in the air and coming down a little steeply; he is learning to 'flatten out', however.

He is more solid than the other Thoroughbreds in the yard and reminds me of Spinning Rhombus; coincidentally he has the same owner, Rosemary Barlow. He was placed in a couple of advanced runs and in both his two-star starts in 1997.

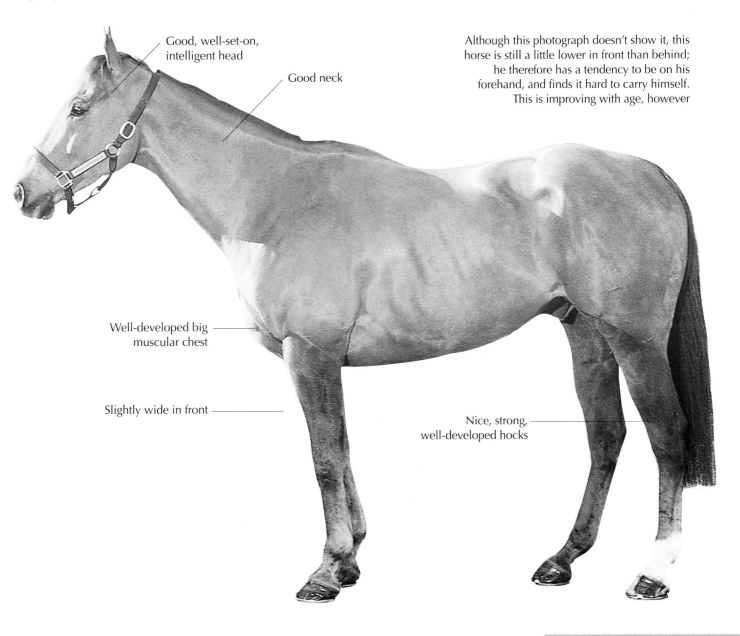

Good, well-set-on, intelligent head

Good neck

Although this photograph doesn't show it, this horse is still a little lower in front than behind; he therefore has a tendency to be on his forehand, and finds it hard to carry himself. This is improving with age, however

Well-developed big muscular chest

Slightly wide in front

Nice, strong, well-developed hocks

Sir Samuel 7yo New Zealand Thoroughbred chestnut stallion, 16.1hh, by Sambuk

He has a good temperament but ultimately he didn't come on as I'd hoped, and I decided he'd have a better future as a gelding, so he was gelded at the end of 1997.

I brought Sir Samuel over to England with the idea of getting him to international level and then standing him at stud. He looks solid because he has the stallion crest, and he is compact, powerful and a good jumper. He is quiet, but intelligent, and he was braver than some stallions: entires are in fact harder to event than people realise because they think and worry about what they are doing more than other horses. A stallion is not ideal as a pure event horse – four-star level is asking a lot of him – but if he stands at stud at a yard different to the one from which he is evented, he should learn to differentiate between the two duties and still behave at competitions.

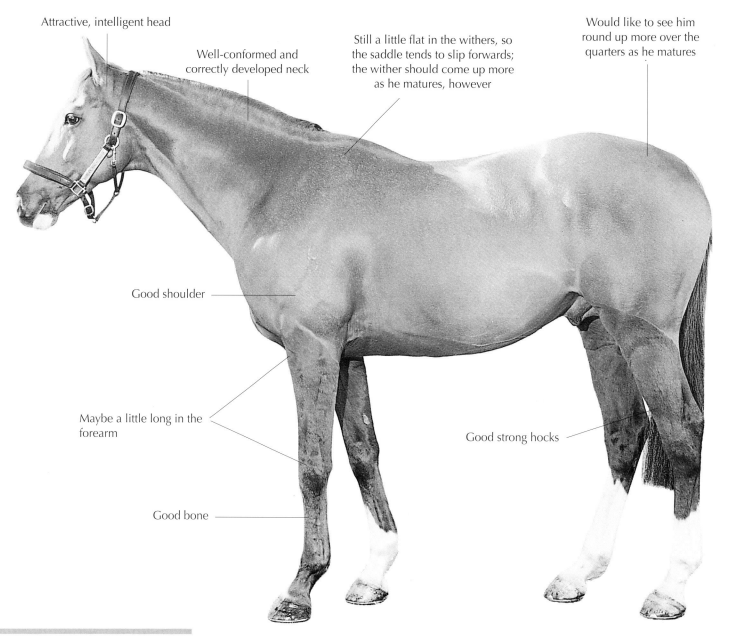

Attractive, intelligent head

Well-conformed and correctly developed neck

Still a little flat in the withers, so the saddle tends to slip forwards; the wither should come up more as he matures, however

Would like to see him round up more over the quarters as he matures

Good shoulder

Maybe a little long in the forearm

Good strong hocks

Good bone

Spinning Rhombus 16yo bay gelding, 15.3hh, by Magic Circle out of Saving Grace

He looked like an insignificant, stuffy pony, but if you could have looked under the bonnet you would have found a V8 engine with a turbo fitted! Proved to be very sound and tough.

This is how Spinning Rhombus used to halt in the dressage! He may not look impressive here, but he was one of the best cross-country horses of all time.

He had a great will to stay on his feet and this led to so many clear rounds – there were occasions when he nearly fell, but somehow he would recover, often when it looked impossible. He went under water at Stockholm once. He completed fourteen three-day events, and earned nearly 1,000 points.

Alert, tough head, but with small, mean, rebellious eyes

Lower in front than behind: he therefore tended to be on his forehand and found self-carriage hard

Well-shaped back and body

Strong hindquarters

'Stood over' in front

Deep girth

Nice, short cannon bones and good bone below the knee

CROSS-COUNTRY SCHOOLING

Practising at home

Our young horses' first introduction to cross-country will always be at home in familiar surroundings, using 'home-made' fences and combinations fashioned out of showjumping poles.

   The horse I am riding in the session on the pages which follow is All Honour; he was bought straight out of the sale ring as a three-year-old at Doncaster, having been raced a few times. He was 'nagged on' at home whenever anyone had a spare few weeks to ride him, and he started proper work in December, three months before this schooling session. He had, of course, done some gridwork and straightforward jumping over poles, but he had never seen combinations before. The aim was not to get him performing like a ready-made Grand Prix showjumper, but to gain his confidence and to teach him to look at what he was doing before he encountered real cross-country fences.

A typical Nicholson training session: everyone permanently on the move, relaxed and having fun

   I am not a great believer in having to work at making a youngster jump off his hocks – I feel that some riders work their horses too hard at home with endless gridwork to try and turn them into snappy jumpers – instead I am more interested in them finding their own balance, and I find that most of them improve dramatically once they are competing. Besides, some horses will never be able to jump off their hocks, but will always be on the forehand – I don't think this matters because a horse should always go in his own natural way. I hate to see riders yanking their horses about in order to try and change their shape, because to my mind it is much more important that the horse should be left alone to concentrate on what he is doing. Too many riders pressurise their horses at this stage; they seem to forget that a horse has four legs of its own and is perfectly capable of getting from A to B without them trying to help it every stride of the way. Constantly fiddling with a horse's stride or hitting it at random will soon put it off, and you will have problems. The whole idea is that the schooling session should be fun and relaxed.

A practice session with All Honour

To begin with, I canter All Honour backwards and forwards over a simple vertical of about 2ft 6in (70cm) with a clear groundline in order to gain his confidence (1). We then raise the pole to the top of the jump-stand (2) – about 3ft 3in (1m) – and after All Honour has jumped this in both directions I will ride him to and fro over it, making figure-of-eight shapes and coming into it at different angles (3, 4

& 5). We jump the fence in the centre every time, but at an angle of, say, 45 degrees instead of 90.

The basic principle of cross-country riding is to be able to get a horse to jump where you want it to and this exercise is good practice for the rider in holding the horse on a line. It also helps the horse's agility, because you are turning him in as he lands and he is having to do flying

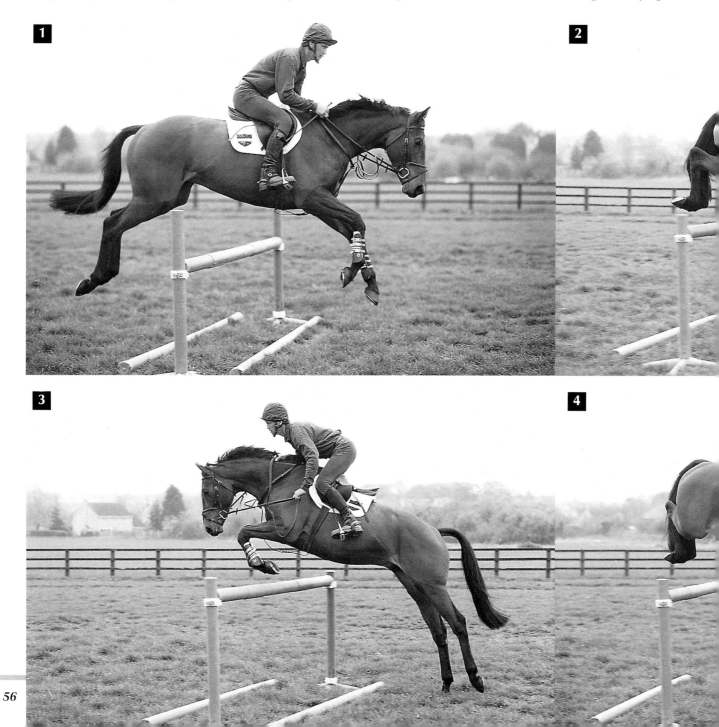

changes – in other words, changing his leading leg as he changes direction. I often do this exercise with my advanced horses to see at how sharp an angle I can take them into a fence.

The next step is to ride straight at the fence again, but aiming to jump it near the edge (5). It is important that low jump-stands are used for this exercise because the whole point is to give the horse the option of running out and then to teach him politely not to. We approach the fence with a nice level stride and an even, firm contact on the mouth. I keep my stick ready in my outside hand in case All Honour wavers – a horse will always react away from the stick-side – and I gently support him with contact on the inside rein.

This exercise is the nearest I will go to practising arrowhead-type fences at home. Not everyone agrees, but I don't think arrowhead practice at home is realistic because there is too much risk of the horse running out – in fact that is often how they get the idea in the first place – and you often end up fighting the horse and winding it up.

5

1

2

CROSS-COUNTRY SCHOOLING

The lesson becomes more exciting when we add a colourful filler tray, which imitates a ditch, placing it *flat*, one stride (6m) away from the upright and laying supporting rails on the ground on either side to help keep the horse straight. All Honour is now quite confident about jumping the vertical, but the filler will surprise him a bit and keep him alert. We approach the rail more positively than before

and he jumps it neatly (1 & 2), then, as anticipated, has a good look at the tray before jumping it (3). The important thing is for the rider neither to get ahead of the movement nor to lean back and hang on to the horse's mouth, but to maintain a secure lower leg and keep a contact with his mouth but without restricting him. Let him look at the filler, but make him realise that he still has to jump it.

4

5

9

8

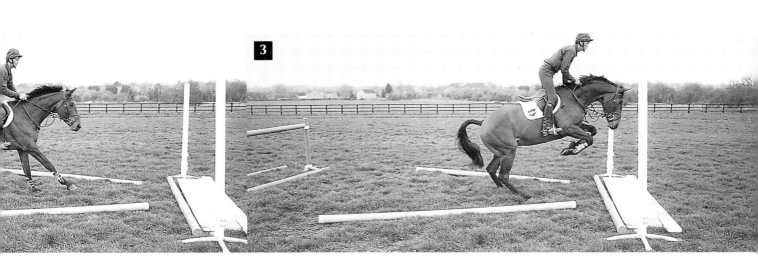

After jumping it backwards and forwards a few times, we take away the supporting rails and move the filler 3m nearer the vertical so that it is now a bounce distance (4–9).

When you approach a new type of fence for the first time, ride the horse positively, because if he is allowed to hesitate there is more chance that he will get in a muddle and leave his hindlegs behind and so frighten himself. It is on the second and subsequent attempts that you should ride more quietly and with a more relaxed contact, because the horse will be more confident. If you ride at *every* fence with terrific gusto you will soon make the horse over-excited, when the whole point is to keep him as calm as possible.

1

2

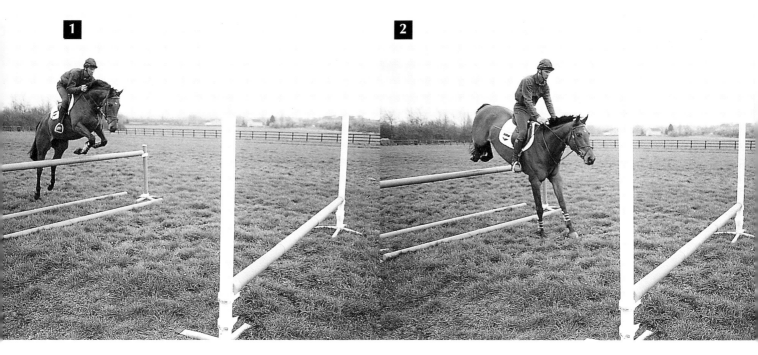

Replace the filler with a rail about a foot high, again at a bounce distance of 8ft (3m) away (1). Having the second rail at a lower eye level will encourage the horse to look behind the vertical and anticipate, the idea being to make him think of more than one obstacle at once. He needs to realise that he has to jump the first rail as well as the second (2–4), although it doesn't matter if he goes through the first one to begin with. This is a good exercise to help the rider to keep a secure leg.

5

6

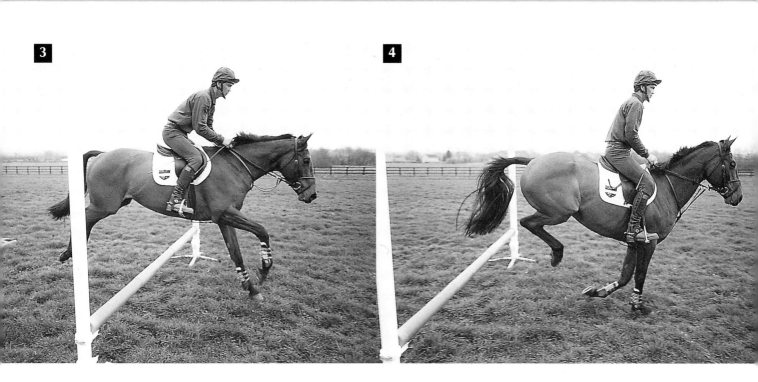

We also introduce All Honour to the idea of a small corner fence, built at milkchurn height – about 2ft (65cm) – and not too wide to begin with – about 2ft 6in (70cm) in the centre (5). We approach it positively, at a strong canter, and as he starts to look at it I wrap my legs around him: although he is allowed to look at the fence, he must realise that he has to keep going (6). As he looks down at the corner he becomes a little underpowered, so I squeeze him firmly on take-off to encourage him to stretch and make the spread (7). Next we jump it backwards and forwards, widening the spread and encouraging him to jump nearer the corner. This exercise is made much easier by the earlier practice of jumping the vertical at the edge. I keep the stick in my outside hand to keep the horse straight.

1   **2**   **3**

Then, for a change, I take All Honour down the centre, aiming to jump over the milkchurn. At first unsure he wavers (1 & 2) and squirms to the left. Repeating the exercise I move the stick that is already in my left hand closer onto his neck and have slightly more bend to the right (3). He jumps very straight and lands well balanced with a confident relaxed expression on his face (4 & 5).

The only form of barrel jumping we do at home is to have three in a row touching each other, and using supporting poles as wings. Many top riders practise 'circus tricks' over single barrels at home, but I once tried it with a horse before I took him to Blenheim, knowing that the course there contains several arrowheads, and when we got to the actual event he ran out at an arrowhead, something he had never done before. The trouble is that one feels so pleased at getting the horse to jump the single barrel once that it's human nature to try it again – and the chances are that he will then run out. I have seen it happen often, and I also know of the odd top rider who frequently jumps single barrels in lecture-demonstrations with a particular horse, and then wonders why it runs out at an actual competition. On a real cross-country course you usually get a 'normal' fence after an arrowhead and, anyway, once the horse has jumped the chevron he will forget about it. At home one is tempted to keep practising, and then the horse will invariably start playing up and running out, which is exactly what All Honour does here (6) – the lesson being that horses are not machines.

The real thing

I usually take a young horse cross-country schooling twice before his first event, although some of them only need to go once, depending on their aptitude. I never used to be a big fan of cross-country schooling – I didn't do any with Spinning Rhombus when he started, but would just take him straight to an event and it wasn't a problem. Nowadays, however, cross-country schooling is more fashionable, and as there are more good courses available locally, I do it quite a lot. I often take a batch of four-year-olds schooling with the older horses. The four-star horses don't go

schooling at the start of the season, but they will certainly go before a major three-day event because, having so many horses to event, it is quite likely that I might not have competed with the horses of that standard for the previous six weeks.

A week after the poles session at home, All Honour had his first proper cross-country schooling lesson, ridden by my working pupil Leonard, who has represented France as a Junior. I took the five-year-old Turtle, who had never seen anything like this before, and my ex-working pupil Pierre joined

2

The first fence (1&2) is always a small log because horses will jump a solid fence more easily. I canter towards it, not worrying too much about seeing a perfect stride because I am more concerned about keeping Turtle going forwards in front of my leg. He looks at the fence, but it doesn't matter because I already have my leg on, squeezing him forwards. Leonard, Pierre and I follow each other over this log a few times, going backwards and forwards over it, and when the horses are jumping it confidently we canter on to the next fence without stopping. The horses gain confidence and enjoyment from following each other, and the continuous cantering between fences helps them to maintain a good rhythm. Stopping and starting is the worst thing you can do us on a six-year-old which had been showjumped but which had also never seen a cross-country fence. We used a nearby course owned by Robin Dumas, beautifully laid out and with a huge variety of fences within just two fields; this means that a young horse is not over-faced with long distances between obstacles. I don't think you need a massive farm for cross-country schooling fences, just a variety of fences in a compact space.

I don't believe in spending ages walking the horse around showing him fences because I think this can be confusing for him, so we warm up by trotting for about twenty metres, then cantering around at a controlled pace, but with more purpose than if it were just a flatwork session; a purposeful canter lets the horse know that he is here for a different job than just to go around in a circle in the school at home looking pretty. We follow each other cantering around the jumps and changing the rein, but only for a couple of minutes because we don't want to wear the horses out before we start. It is important to teach a young horse while he is alert and not tired or bored: both Turtle and All Honour had raced on the flat as three-year-olds so their stamina levels were quite well developed, but if a horse begins to feel tired, either physically or mentally, you should stop the session immediately before he makes a mistake and becomes frightened.

with a young horse at this stage because it ruins his rhythm and may worry him into thinking that a fence might be a potential problem. If you can keep a horse's confidence and ensure that he enjoys himself, there is no reason why he should stop at a new type of fence.

It is important not to apply too much pressure on the horse's mouth between jumps because at this stage we should not be forcing a young horse into an outline. Every horse likes to go a little differently and I think it is a big mistake to try to alter his individual, natural way of going because this can interfere with his balance. I like to let a horse approach a fence as he would if he were galloping around a field by himself.

The next stage after the single ditch is a coffin (1), although we will have cantered on over an easier fence in between to keep up the youngsters' confidence. It is important to intersperse complex fences with plain ones, and I would not, for instance, jump a coffin twice in succession with a young horse. When tackling a coffin it is important to keep riding into it because the horse will definitely look into the ditch – you *must* therefore keep moving into the first rail, or he will have too much time to be surprised by the ditch and then he will stop. Turtle jumped the first rail neatly. I loosen his head a little, and as he has a good look at the ditch (2), I squeeze his ribs with my legs, sitting still, looking ahead and keeping him going forwards and out over the final rail (4 & 5).

We jump two or three plain fences and then canter directly to a small ditch (1). Again, the same theory applies: always have the horse in front of your leg. It's a sure bet that Turtle will look into the ditch, so I apply a little bit of stronger leg pressure and make up his mind for him. Leave the head loose so that the horse can look down and the rider doesn't get pulled forward. With a young horse, stick to small ditches; they can easily become over-faced by too wide or deep a ditch, and this can lead to problems later on in competition.

All Honour jumps confidently into the coffin with Leonard, but then he sees the ditch and 'props' into it (1); even so, he jumps it quite well, though his style lacks impetus (2) and he gets a bit unbalanced approaching the final element (3). One leg hangs down, but the pair stays out of trouble because Leonard sits still and in balance with a secure leg around the girth, thus allowing All Honour to correct his own balance.

The next, easier test is a small trakehner, which is approached in the same way as the other fences – in other words, in a positive canter (1). I anticipate that Turtle will want to look down into the ditch, and I have my leg ready to make up his mind for him and squeeze him up to jump (2). Turtle jumps this quite low in comparison to Pierre's horse (3), which has had more of a look and 'showjumps' it.

We move on to a bank, where the aim is to train the horses to jump up-and downhill. First we teach them just to jump up onto a bank, still from that continuous canter. We turn around at the top, cantering all the time, and jump back off. Horses usually try to come back to a trot or even a walk on a bank, but my aim is always to keep them cantering.

Next we try a more difficult combination where the horse has to land, balance on the bank and jump over a rail. Turtle is not quite sure about this, as you can see from his approach (1), so I latch my legs around him and propel him forwards to the front of the bank, keeping the same even, light contact on his mouth as he lands on top of the bank (2 & 3). I sit a little more strongly into the saddle and press him with my legs to encourage him to jump off the bank, making sure as I get in behind him that I do *not* pull on the reins and catch his mouth (4 & 5).

Pierre's horse reacts in typical youngster fashion: he nearly runs out (6) and his legs dangle everywhere (7), but Pierre manages to keep *his* leg on and so keeps the horse going forwards (8).

1

After jumping a few more island fences, the next excitement is a corner. As in the poles session at home, the idea is to canter straight at it as though I am jumping a parallel, making sure that I maintain even pressure in each hand to stop the horse running out. What I like about All Honour's performance here is that although he looks, he is able to pull himself up in mid-air and extend over the corner, and Leonard makes him jump from where *he* wants (2).

2

It is now time for a breather! We have probably jumped sixty times over about twenty different types of fence without stopping, and it is time to rest and walk the horses about for five minutes. I realise that not everyone conducts their cross-country schooling in this way, and some people might consider it a somewhat haphazard and hair-raising method! However I personally believe that continuous riding in between fences at a relaxed pace is the best way to get a horse ready to achieve a nice rhythm; I find that it makes them much easier to ride and it sharpens them up. I want the horse's adrenalin to be up and for him to be thinking all the time, even though we are not charging about at high speed.

Now it is time for the water challenge. First we introduce the horses to the idea by trotting down a gentle slope into the water, being ready to encourage them in if they start to look and want to go backwards. It is important not to creep up to water as if it is something of which to be frightened. I walk and trot the horses around in the water for a while, and then trot back up the bank and out onto dry land again. Then I turn and canter towards the water, aiming to jump in off a small bank (1). Turtle backs off and hesitates, but the forward impetus gets him into the water. In the same way as the bank exercise, freedom of rein is important, and I also keep my upper body back in case the drag of the water unbalances the horse. Turtle

skews a bit, but I let him have the freedom of his head so I can keep behind him because I don't want him to land and drop to a walk – it is important to keep going (2&3).

Pierre's horse doesn't back off at all and canters straight in confidently, but misses his footing as he lands (4). Pierre forgets all about style and concentrates on self-preservation – he obviously learnt something from his spell in the Nicholson yard! – and, sure enough, it all comes back together again. Pierre manages not to haul his horse's teeth out, and as a result, the horse has the freedom of his neck and can use his head to re-balance himself (5).

After this excitement, we jump half-a-dozen more island fences on the way to a set of steps, which will be the last exercise. First we descend the steps, approaching from a canter (6). I make sure that my upper body is behind the movement so that as Turtle starts to look and prop, I'm already in the right place to prompt him and give him confidence (7). Turtle carries on and jumps happily down the steps (8). As regards the riding, it is not just a case of my sitting there and letting it all happen: you must repeat the process of sitting behind the movement, all the time continuing to press the horse onwards. I slip the reins, at the same time keeping contact with Turtle's mouth though being careful not to hang on to the mouth, because if I did he might pull me forward, and if he pecked I would have a good chance of disappearing out of the front door.

We turn around at the bottom and canter back up the steps, applying the same principle as coming down. As you jump up the first step, keep pressing upwards to the second and third (9). This is a useful exercise in improving a horse's balance, and these horses found it easy after doing the bank and water complexes. It is a good note on which to end the school session, in which the principal aim must always be for everyone to have fun, and to feel confident and relaxed.

What to do when it doesn't go according to plan

Although this particular schooling session went very well, with Turtle jumping confidently throughout, if at any stage he had felt as though he might get confused and risk having a fall, I would have pulled up. Sometimes young horses start to feel brain-tired and it can be dangerous to continue to push them. A horse can only learn while its brain is functioning clearly. Turtle had already done a lot of jumping over poles at home, and on this occasion he was enjoying himself and I didn't have to work too hard; but even if he had been less confident, I wouldn't keep stopping and starting him and fiddling around waiting for him to feel exactly right in his approach to a fence, I would just keep riding him positively.

Pulling up before a fence is the worst thing you can do with a young horse because it unsettles him – the only sort of jump I'd turn away from if I felt the horse really wasn't right in his approach would be something like a corner or a wide oxer where there was a danger that he could land in the middle. If the fence was a vertical, I would keep going, even if he didn't feel too willing, because he should have done enough jumping at home to be able to stay on his feet.

If you circle a horse away from a fence, you are more likely to have a fall later on, because he will have half his mind on jumping and half on turning away. I am not a big fan of turning circles in front of a fence because not only will the horse start to think backwards, but so will you. Cross-country riding is about confidence and looking forwards.

Occasionally a horse will mess around, bucking and napping, and in such a situation I would always make sure I had it following an older companion: if a horse has a lead, it will get into the habit of jumping first time around. Taking it hunting can be a solution to the problem of nappiness, although I don't ever find the time.

It is also important not to dither around with a potentially nappy horse; if it gets into the habit of getting out of the lorry and being jumped straightaway, it will get used to jumping without thinking about it. The knack is to try and think one step ahead of your horse, and not have it running rings around you instead.

The older horse which has got into the habit of stopping or is a bit chicken – I suppose Buckley Province would come into this category – is much harder to sort out than a spooky youngster who is just being naughty. It doesn't make any difference to me how much experience an older horse has, I would still school it over small fences, riding each one with as much commitment as if I were going around Badminton. You can ride an older horse into a fence with that much more pace because it has enough experience to know where to put its feet and you don't need to allow it the 'looking' period that you do with a youngster.

I never school over big fences because I don't think it works in cold blood. Even with a Badminton horse, the week before the competition I will take him schooling over small fences in order to remind him that jumping is both fun and easy.

I was given Cartoon to ride because he had tipped up a few times with his previous partner Pippa Funnell. He actually won his first three advanced events with me and I suppose everyone thought I had instantly cracked it, but in fact he made a horrendous mistake every time out and I very nearly fell off him on each occasion. Although he doesn't have a great technique – his legs dangle about – he is a very genuine horse who never thinks of stopping, and the answer with him is to take a softer approach. I have got to know him better and realise that I was probably riding him too strongly at first.

With a horse that rushes its fences the important thing is neither to fight to slow the horse down, nor to let go of the reins. You need to keep your hands and body completely still, neither leaning back nor forwards; at first you will probably meet fences faster than you might like, but the horse should get the message after a while. A rushing horse should be schooled over fences with a good groundline – certainly not an upright like a gate – and you must train yourself to sit still and wait for the obstacle. If you fight the horse, it'll chuck its head up and won't look where it's going – and you won't see too much yourself through an eyeful of ear and mane!

A few years ago I rode a horse called Kingscourt, who had a reputation for rushing. The first time I rode him at an event, Paddy Muir, who used to ride him, called out: 'Do you want a card or flowers?' About two seconds later Kingscourt had chucked his head in the air over a practice fence and broken his noseband. As there was only one minute before I was due to go across country, I just had to stuff the noseband in my pocket and hope for the best. I think we were actually placed on that occasion, and in fact we had quite a bit of success together. I learned to leave him alone, but he was always a bit erratic.

A constantly pulling horse is much harder to ride because as it lands it will be so quickly away that in a combination fence you'll find yourself right on top of the second element. Jagermeister sometimes does this, although he gets away with it because he's a very good jumper. All I can do with him is to sit as still as I can when he lands and try and slow him down to a safe speed. If I fight him, he will throw his head in the air, so the only thing I can do is to keep a quiet but firm hold on the reins and try and slow his pace – if I just let him run on it would be dangerous. I try not to resort to the short-term easier option of putting a big bit in a pulling horse's mouth – although it is often the only answer for a small girl riding a big strong horse.

If a horse has a bad, shaking fall at a competition, I always take it schooling over small fences, unless it had a fall as a result of being too brave – that often makes them easier to rider afterwards! A session over small fences will help a horse to get its confidence back, and I make sure that we have company. I can't stress enough the importance of schooling in company; a lot of people make the mistake of going by themselves, and then as soon as something goes slightly wrong they start hesitating and the damage is done. Your own confidence is as important as that of the horse.

CROSS-COUNTRY ACTION

You don't necessarily need a horse who is a superstar or very expensive to be successful and have fun in the cross-country phase. Generally, horses love it – or at least you can teach and encourage them to love it. I never cease to be rewarded and delighted by the will of the horse to get to the other side of the fence.

A horse doesn't have to be a top athlete to go well across country – you can achieve good results with a moderate horse both through training and through giving it confidence. Even at four-star level – at events such as Badminton and Burghley – where the fences may look enormous to you, the horse who has confidence will find them very easy.

It's amazing the number of horses we've had who we didn't think would make it past novice level. Applause, a horse we used to own, springs to mind, but if you look at the photographs of him in the next few pages you will see how easy he makes it look. Spinning Rhombus also started at the same time and was even less promising, but he went on to become one of the most reliable and best cross-country horses ever.

Amazingly – and despite photographer Kit Houghton's best efforts! – there are no pictures of me hitting the deck in this chapter, which is surprising, considering that I think I fell off more times during the 1997 season than in my entire career. I had one particularly bad spate in the summer, but miraculously there were no photographers about! (On one occasion, when I had actually bashed my leg rather painfully, the doctor on duty showed great concern about the state of my nose – he didn't really believe me when I told him it had been like that since I was three!)

It is a fact of life in eventing that you will have to put up with the odd fall, but try not to worry about it too much. Even the best horses will give you the occasional fall and, as long as no one is hurt, it's no big deal and it shouldn't put you off a horse. It might even be a good thing if either you or the horse has become over-confident. I had a bit of a crash, although thankfully a harmless one, last year on Merillion. He came to me a couple of months previously with a reputation for pulling and being headstrong and, quite frankly, the fall did him no harm at all. Dawdle is one of the best horses I have at the moment, but we once had a fall at Saumur when I was sailing along mentally counting the prize money. It was annoying, but it probably did both him and me some good. What I hope the following pictures will show is that horses will always surprise you; one of the most important attributes for cross-country riding is an ability to be ready for anything. There is a very fine line between triumph and disaster and, inevitably, things will go wrong. Even the best horses slip, get confused or miss strides. And it isn't necessarily the most stylish riders who have the foot-perfect rounds on the most talented horses who will win. The most successful cross-country riders are the alert and well-prepared ones who can react quickly and calmly in the face of a potential mishap and rescue the situation.

BIG TABLE SPREAD ON HIGHLY RATED

This enormous table spread on a slight downhill run was at Savernake in 1997 – Highly Rated is a big horse and you can't see much of him in the photograph as we approach the fence. Although this type of island fence is theoretically classed as a 'let-up' in between more technical questions, it doesn't mean that you can switch off and leave it to the horse. It is important to make jumping this type of fence as easy as possible for the horse so that he enjoys it, rather than struggling over it and frightening himself because you have let him take off too far out. I keep the pressure on Highly Rated going into the fence and don't let him take off too early. Even so, because he is a careful jumper, he flicks his hindlegs to make sure he doesn't hit it and this makes him slightly pitch on landing.

DRAWBRIDGE ON STRATEGY

This fence at Punchestown in 1994 was the ultimate rider-frightener and, unsurprisingly, it was created by the ingenious Irish designer Tommy Brennan. The horses had to jump off the drawbridge over a very wide gap onto an island where there was a short one-stride distance into the water. There was considerable nervousness about this fence and we were all convinced that the horses would fall down the gap. It was a first three-star level three-day event for Strategy, who was later sold to Frenchman Cedric Lyard, and we were first on the course. I galloped flat out at it; Strategy jumped boldly off the drawbridge and bounced into the water, whereas some of the more experienced horses managed to shuffle a little stride. This fence caused very little trouble in the end and it was the way out of the water which actually caused more problems.

COGNAC GLASS ON OPTIMIST

This fence was designed for the benefit of the sponsor of Burghley, which in 1993 was Remy Martin, and although it is just a single island fence on the way home, it wasn't one at which you'd want to take a flyer. An upright fence which has high sides should be approached with respect, as you would a gate in the showjumping arena, and on an even stride, not on a long flat one.

ELEPHANT TRAP ON APPLAUSE

This picture was taken at Bramham in 1991. I try to ride at elephant traps as if the ditch isn't there – it is absolutely crucial not to look down and get unnerved by the ditch. If a horse really doesn't like ditches, this type of fence could be its undoing at the higher levels of competition, and it tends to be psychologically difficult for riders. The more I worry about the ditch, the worse it gets, so I try to maintain a strong, even rhythm, pretending the ditch isn't there, and if I can do that, things tend to go better. The main thing is not to let go of the horse's head and flap the reins because that will encourage it to look down.

DITCH AND BRUSH ON APPLAUSE

Applause, whom I later sold to Mandy Stibbe, was one of the fastest horses I've ever had – his nickname was Speedy. This fence, the famous Centaur's Leap at Burghley, is quite awesome when you first see it, but I think riders are pretty used to it by now. Again, I ride at it as if there is no ditch. Applause was also a careful horse and he is making sure he gets high over the brush. That year, 1991, Applause went on to give me my first good placing at Burghley, sixth.

POINTE NOIRE AT AN AIRY LOG

A week before this picture was taken at Hartpury, Pointe Noire gave me a bit of a shock at a similar fence at Iping, when he got his front feet over it and then somehow managed to whip around backwards so he was facing the other way. I warned Kit Houghton that this could be an exciting fence for him to photograph with this young horse, and as I approached it I wanted to laugh because I could see Kit crouching with eager anticipation! To my surprise, however, it was completely incident free.

I knew the approach would be important, as Pointe Noire, who belongs to Rosemary Barlow, was quite inexperienced for an advanced course of this calibre and I wanted to make sure we had no trouble this time. I rode at the log in a powerful but controlled canter, as if it was a treble in the showjumping arena, and for the last five strides kept my leg pressed on strongly and kept hold of the horse's head. I didn't start to sit up until he took off, because I didn't want him to stop, so I sat up gradually to enable him to carry the jump through, and I'm amazed by how smooth it looks.

PIMPLE FENCE ON CARTOON

With this type of narrow fence it is important to pick your line from a long way out and to commit the horse to it. Press the horse up into your hand, apply plenty of even leg pressure, maintain a secure contact on the rein, keeping the horse's head still, and it will simply not be in a position to veer left or right. The pimple fence has become popular with course designers in recent years; it pressurises the rider into getting the horse straight in advance – you haven't a hope of suddenly correcting your line at the last minute. Cartoon is usually a very honest horse; he is far more experienced than Sir Samuel, pictured at a pimple fence opposite, and he is quite easy to ride, so this fence at Bramham was no problem to him – in fact he went on to take second place. The fence also came off a turn, which made it easier. There was then one stride to a seat, but provided you'd cleared the pimple, you couldn't go far wrong here. However, my second ride, Erica Watson's Romanov, stalled, got stuck on top of the pimple and incurred 20 penalties!

PIMPLE FENCE
WITH SIR SAMUEL

This narrow vertical fence is on a downhill slope and follows the bank at Aldon (pictured on pages 90–1 with Just Zulu). Sir Samuel, another stallion, was having his first intermediate run and I must have felt that he was travelling too fast in a long, flat shape because I am trying to slow him down with a fairly drastic half-halt (1). But by the time he takes off, he has lowered his head to look at the fence and jumps it neatly (2 & 3).

DOG-LEG FENCE ON ALL HONOUR

This narrow fence is near the end of the course at Portman Horse Trials and is approached up a sharp incline, with one stride on flat ground before jumping. It was All Honour's first outing, but he had gone so boldly around the rest of the course that I decided to take the direct route. He *felt* confident to me, but as you can see from the first picture, he was surprised to see the jump and looks unsure. We had approached the fence at a powerful, controlled canter, which makes it easier to keep him straight, and I wrapped my legs around him and pushed him on. All Honour went on to complete a nice, confident clear round.

BULLFINCH COMBINATION ON ALL BLACK

This combination of a plain brush fence with one stride to a bullfinch at Bicton came on the last novice outing for All Black, Jo and Charles Collins' home-bred horse, before he upgraded to intermediate. I ride the last few strides more positively because I am expecting All Black to back off from the bullfinch, as most horses would. He jumps the first part well and as he lands I ride him forwards to the bullfinch, where he dives to the right but still jumps confidently through the branches, which are quite thick.

It is important to ride positively at a bullfinch, even on an experienced horse, because otherwise they will stop and 'balloon' over it rather than jumping *through* the brush.

3

2

A BANK WITH JUST ZULU

The important thing here is to let the bank come to you, rather than the other way round. Don't get in front of the movement, and let the horse jump onto it cleanly (1). As Just Zulu moves to jump off this bank at Aldon Horse Trials, I stay behind the movement (4). My body is just behind the centre of gravity but I am not restricting his head so that he can see where to land and isn't jumping wildly into space. It is a downhill landing, so I sit still and let Zulu regain his balance and look for the next fence (5). Zulu is a stallion and they tend to be more cautious and careful of their undercarriage. You can't bully a stallion, so you have to let him look, while simultaneously reassuring him that the fence is OK.

5

STAIRCASE WITH WHIT MONDAY

This complex comes straight after the first water at Aldon and consists of three big steps – one stride to the second and a bounce to the third – on a slight curve. Whit Monday stands 17.3hh and is the biggest horse in the yard, and it is difficult to maintain impulsion when he loses power. He probably came out of the water more slowly than the smaller horses and he therefore takes off quite a long way back from the first step, only just making it. However, rather than trying to make him shorten in front of the bank, which would lose more power, I keep him going forwards. Approaching the second step, I loosen his head and try to drive him forwards (2). He only just makes that step as well with his hindlegs (3), and in order to make the final step, I have to help his front end up by applying pressure to his mouth (4). It might not look immaculate, but at least he's got his ears pricked!

93

NEW YORK AT THE BEAUFORT DITCH/COFFIN

This coffin-type complex comes very quickly after the water at Gatcombe and is the last difficult test; it could almost be renamed 'Andrew's Ditch' considering the number of times I have landed in it! It necessitates a very sharp turn if you are going to take the direct route through it inside the tree (1), as we do here, and the line taken means that we have to jump the first element on an angle (2). It is then a short one stride down a slight slope to a ditch and brush fence.

I look as if I'm grabbing hold of New York and moving him along quite strongly because he was going to take off too far back and I wanted him to get in deeper (4). If you're not on a particularly good stride, it is usually wiser to move the horse up to the fence, rather than backing off, although it can be easier said than done! I'm not wearing spurs because New York can get quite keen enough, and his martingale is done up quite tightly, compared to Cartoon's, which gives me a bit more control. He is so big that he can get away with taking strides out, but this is something I prefer young horses not to do.

New York is New Zealand-bred, and was first produced by a rider out there called Gee Davidson; Gee also produced a good horse called Arakai, who is currently being ridden successfully by Ian Stark.

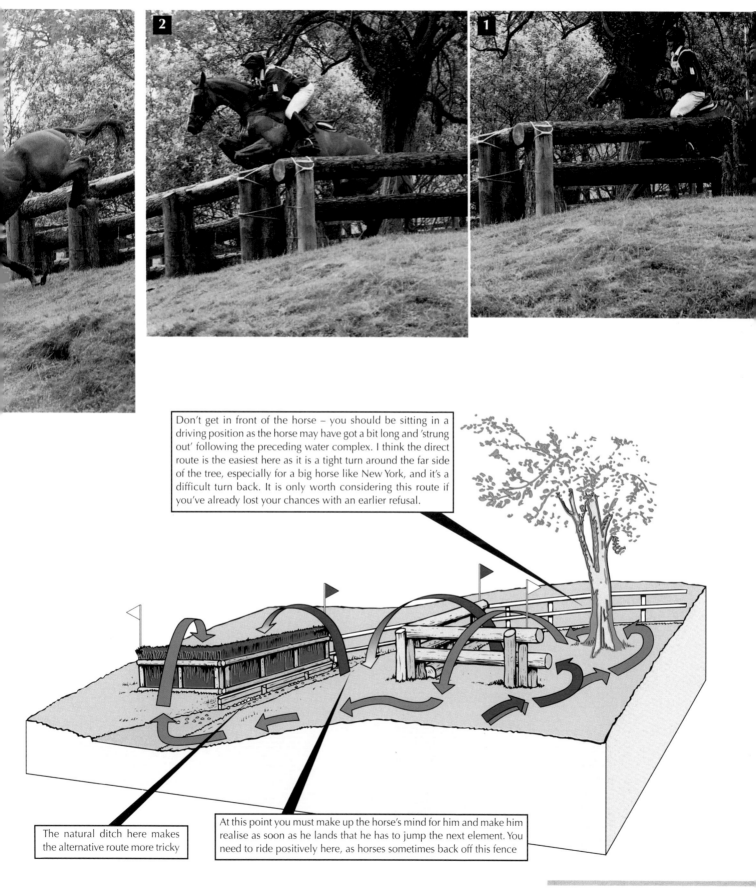

2

1

Don't get in front of the horse – you should be sitting in a driving position as the horse may have got a bit long and 'strung out' following the preceding water complex. I think the direct route is the easiest here as it is a tight turn around the far side of the tree, especially for a big horse like New York, and it's a difficult turn back. It is only worth considering this route if you've already lost your chances with an earlier refusal.

The natural ditch here makes the alternative route more tricky

At this point you must make up the horse's mind for him and make him realise as soon as he lands that he has to jump the next element. You need to ride positively here, as horses sometimes back off this fence

BOUNCE FENCE ON BUCKLEY PROVINCE

This complex involves landing over the first element on to higher ground than the take-off and then bouncing out over a higher vertical with a drop. Buck has seen this fence at Ston Easton three times before in previous years

and he does a neat job, which is what I would expect, considering his experience. I keep him moving up to the fence (1 & 2) and then sit still with my legs secure while waiting for him to jump the second element (3 & 4). I keep my body weight back for the drop and maintain contact on the horse's mouth but without giving him a backward pull. If you pull on the horse's mouth at this stage, it encourages him to rub his stifle over the fence rather than push off with his hindlegs.

DOUBLE OF VERTICALS ON VALHALLA

If you've jumped the first part right, the second part should happen naturally

Pick the place where you want to jump the first element well before you get to the fence. Jumping straight across the two fences is probably the easiest, especially as it is on a downhill line, but remember to keep your eye on the route before you jump the first fence. If the horse leaves a leg behind, you'll be better placed to correct your line

If you choose to make the wider turn, don't pull the horse's head around hard so that it slips, or takes its eye off the fence

This double of verticals in the open novice class at Savernake is reminiscent of the earlier schooling exercises at home with youngsters, and if a horse is practised in jumping angled verticals in the schooling arena, he should have no problem here. There is about three strides in between the two fences, and the second one may have to be taken on the angle after a left-handed turn; or you can angle the first vertical, as I have done, thus making your approach to the second one straighter. Valhalla had just upgraded to intermediate and, as you can see, he is quite confident about jumping angled verticals. Before the fence, I bring him back to a showjumping-type canter, on a shorter, bouncier stride, and keep my eyes fixed on my line; as long as the horse is in a nice, controlled canter approaching a fence like this, it doesn't matter if you don't have the perfect stride – it is more important to have him balanced than to fiddle with his head, thus taking his eyes off the fences, in an effort to get the perfect three strides.

DOUBLE OF CORNERS ON MERILLION

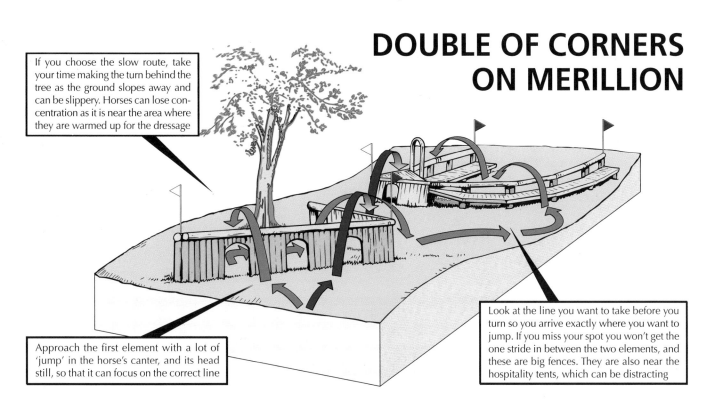

If you choose the slow route, take your time making the turn behind the tree as the ground slopes away and can be slippery. Horses can lose concentration as it is near the area where they are warmed up for the dressage

Approach the first element with a lot of 'jump' in the horse's canter, and its head still, so that it can focus on the correct line

Look at the line you want to take before you turn so you arrive exactly where you want to jump. If you miss your spot you won't get the one stride in between the two elements, and these are big fences. They are also near the hospitality tents, which can be distracting

This was my first three-day event run with Merillion, who had only come to me from Matt Ryan a couple of months previously. Merillion is a very strong ride and by this stage of the course he had started to feel erratic. This double of corners at Bramham, which has a downhill approach and an uphill exit, has a short two-strides distance in between and, because Merillion is a fast horse over jumps, I was aiming to get him to take off quite deep into the first corner so that he would land over it a little short and therefore have room to fit in the two strides.

I pointed him at the first corner at a point where it is quite wide (1) and not exactly in a direct line with the second corner so that I have to turn him towards it. This gives Merillion enough space for two strides and he negotiates the complex well. Although this obstacle is a two-part complex, in this case I found it easier to treat the two elements as separate fences.

PARALLEL BOUNCE ON SPINNING RHOMBUS

I had read in a magazine preview of the 1993 course at Burghley that there was going to be a parallel bounce, so I built a makeshift one at home to practise on Optimist, my second ride. Optimist jumped my home-made model very easily but I wasn't prepared to try it with Spinning

Rhombus because I didn't have much faith that he would be able to do it and I decided not to frighten myself in advance! However, Spinning Rhombus was, as he quite often was, number one on the course and to my surprise he jumped it very easily, whereas later on Optimist struggled a bit. The plan was to approach it with plenty of power and although Spinning Rhombus looks as if he has to stretch over the first element (1), he again shows a deceptive amount of scope because he actually lands well in the middle of the combination (2) and has the power to hop out neatly.

DOWNHILL BOUNCE ON POLKERRIS

This fence came near the end of the course at Le Lion d'Angers in 1991, which is a very good two-star level three-day event in France where many good horses, including Spinning Rhombus, started their careers. This combination came on a downhill slope and was approached out of woodland. When I walked it, I couldn't decide whether it was a one-stride or a bounce distance, so I rode it on a forward stride. The important thing was to sit still and present the horse on an even stride, giving him enough power in his stride so that he can do what he wants. Most horses, including Polkerris, bounced it easily. However, having jumped this fence, the drama is far from over because there is a steep, slippery turn to be negotiated immediately afterwards and if you're not in control, you risk shooting over the ropes into the crowds.

BOMB CRATER ON HIGHLY RATED

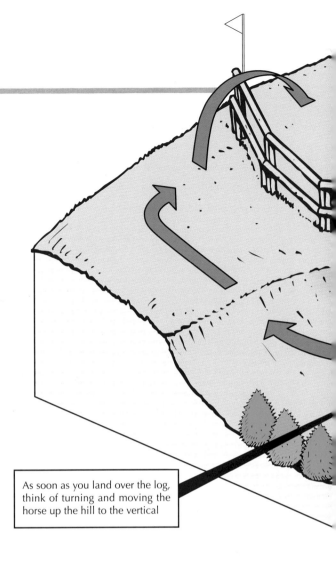

This two-part complex at Savernake started with a log which had an 'into space' effect, as horses landed in a dip, the 'crater'. That in itself wasn't particularly difficult, but you had to maintain enough control to make a sharp turn in the bottom of the crater, run up a slope and jump a rail which has been angled away from you in such a way as to make it tempting for the horse to run out. As you can see, I seem to be making a rather drastic turn (4) but it was more important to hold the horse on the line than to worry what I looked like for the photographer! And once we've turned, Highly Rated jumps the rail smoothly (5). This is a cleverly designed fence by Mike Etherington-Smith because his little line of fir trees (3), which is situated close to one log, prevents the rider making a wider turn to the rail.

As soon as you land over the log, think of turning and moving the horse up the hill to the vertical

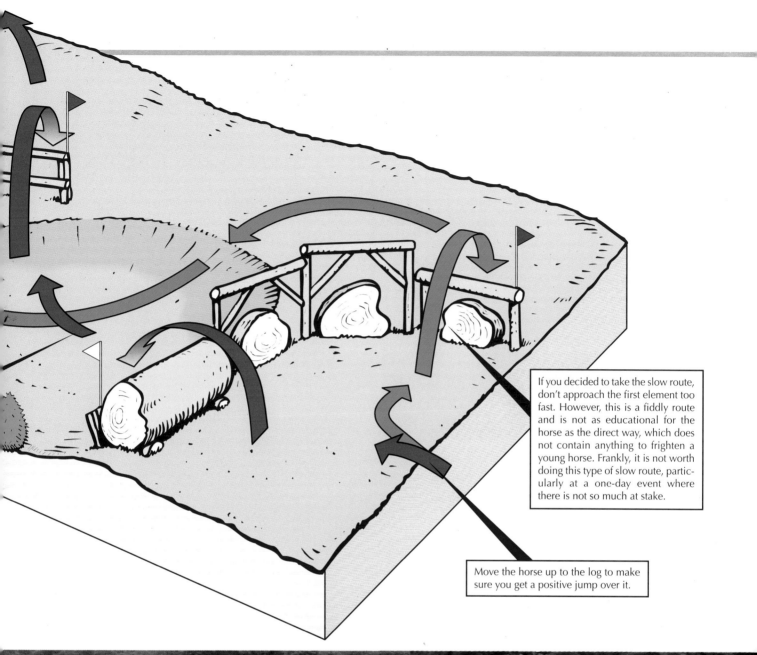

If you decided to take the slow route, don't approach the first element too fast. However, this is a fiddly route and is not as educational for the horse as the direct way, which does not contain anything to frighten a young horse. Frankly, it is not worth doing this type of slow route, particularly at a one-day event where there is not so much at stake.

Move the horse up to the log to make sure you get a positive jump over it.

CARTOON AT A TREBLE OF DROPS

This steep treble of drops is near the end of the British Open course at Gatcombe Park and follows a steep climb uphill which can make horses run out of puff. The landing of the first element is on flat ground, but it gives the impression of being an 'into-space' fence, and the horse can only see the flat ground as he takes off. Then there is one stride before he must launch off a very steep drop, and a bounce to a brush where the landing slopes away sharply.

This is a difficult fence for an inexperienced horse. It is important not to approach it too fast, but make sure you are going forwards enough so that the horse doesn't stop halfway. If you are too slow, you won't have the power to jump.

A good cross-country horse learns to look but not stop, and Cartoon, who is an honest horse, takes off very deliberately but willingly (1). But, this is just the sort of fence at which he tends not to get very high – he had already given me a heart-

stopping moment at a drop earlier on the course – and I'm looking extremely relieved to have got over this part safely (2)! He feels as if he knows what to do, but I still keep thinking forwards, committing both the horse and myself to going, but not letting my bodyweight come forward (3 & 4).

Riders' positions vary in these circumstances, depending on what feels safe for them. Some stick their legs right forwards and lean back up the horse's rump, but I personally feel that this can give a horse negative vibes, and I like to try and make him feel as if I'm jumping the jump, too (5). However, as you can see, I also tend to balance by taking one hand off the reins (6) – and have been known to let go of both! Everyone is different.

You should give the horse the freedom of its head so it can balance, but don't throw the reins at it. You can see as Cartoon moves away from the third fence that he is using his head to balance rather like a rocking-horse (7).

We land on the steep hill down to the water, so the moment we land, I am gathering up Cartoon's reins without interfering with his balance. The first few strides can be used to regain balance and a bit of momentum while thinking about keeping an even stride down the hill.

CARTOON AT COUTTS CORNER

Get the horse back on its hocks as it jumps the palisade and fix your eye on the next fence

If, as you land, you don't feel that you're in complete control, you can keep turning and take the alternative route at the first corner. Also, as these fences are numbered separately, you are allowed to circle in front of it

This is one of the most influential combinations on the course for the British Open Championships at Gatcombe. It is cunningly placed midway on the course, which is the stage at which you've got your horse really galloping and flowing along, and then suddenly you've got to be in control.

In 1997 there was a downhill run to a palisade spread (1), which is followed by an almost 90-degree turn to a wide corner (3), followed by a gentler curve to another substantial corner (5). Some riders took the palisade at an angle, pointing away from the turn, and then swung round back towards the corners; but I wanted to jump it straight, because I find it easier to turn a horse if it can sight the next jump and gradually turn on each stride. A horse who knows his job will be looking for the next fence, so don't confuse him by turning him away.

We approached the palisade at a controlled showjumping canter, and as Cartoon leaves the ground, I start thinking of turning. This is one of my favourite pictures (1); although Cartoon's legs sometimes dangle, he always looks elegant. I then turn him gently on each stride (2), letting him see the first corner gradually. He looks as if he might run out but he is just finishing the turn and, as you can see, he jumps the corners very well.

As you jump the first corner, keep your eyes fixed on the next

DOUBLE OF CORNERS ON WHIT MONDAY

The modern design of filling in corner fences, as seen with this pair at the end of the course at Windsor three-day event, makes them much easier to ride because you can offer the horse a wider bit to jump and if they drop a leg they won't come to any harm. This complex was, therefore, quite inviting and it did not cause too much trouble.

The approach is off a bend, which is a great help, especially if you are nearing the end of the course and the horse is becoming low in front, because you can use the turn to lift the horse's front end without having to pull it about. As we come out of the turn, I gently move Whit Monday up to the fence and this helps to keep him straight. I was very pleased with his round, after which we finished in eighth place on our dressage score.

TRIPLE BRUSH ON JAGERMEISTER

Mark Phillips usually sorts the riders out by building a testing combination at fence 5 for the British Open Championships at Gatcombe Park, and 1996 was no exception. This time he designed a series of arrowhead brushes, all of which had narrow faces but wide spreads, and the complex certainly caused a bit of trouble. Cross-country speed is always a crucial factor at Gatcombe and Mark makes sure that any alternative route is time-consuming.

An arrowhead brush is one of the hardest types of fence to jump and you need to treat it with the utmost respect which, as you can see, Jagermeister doesn't do! He usually launches himself at any fence like a missile and never looks around and I still don't really know what happened here, but as you can see he left it until the last moment to cock his jaw and shoot past. I must have come around the preceding corner quite sharply to save time, and Jagermeister just decided to save even *more* time by not bothering with one of the fences at all!

On my next horse, Dawdle, who was better placed, I opted for the more cautious winding route in view of the nice prize money which was at stake, and in the end we duly finished third behind Mary King's two horses.

Because the spread on this type of fence is so wide, you must commit the horse to it on a forward stride but at the same time, as with all narrow fences, hold him firmly between your leg and hand to prevent him running out.

The theory just didn't quite come off here!

WATER CROSSING WITH WHIT MONDAY

Here at Aldon Horse Trials we jump two logs with a stride in between, the second of which has a fair drop into water; this is followed by a bank and a stride to a rail – a pretty hectic combination for a big horse. The complex also comes off a tight turn and this big horse has already lost impulsion, so as we get over the first log I am reaching for the 'turbo' button (2). I think 'forward' and have my bodyweight a fraction behind the movement in order to push Whit Monday

forwards and make him commit himself to the second log (3). He is a bit far off at take-off and lands steeply in the water (4), but he has jumped confidently, and in slithering over the log, he doesn't frighten himself. My reins are a bit long, but rather than gather them up, I leave his head alone, sit still – and pray!

Whit Monday is a very different horse to ride at a three-day event when there is more galloping and you're not forever pushing him back into his stride.

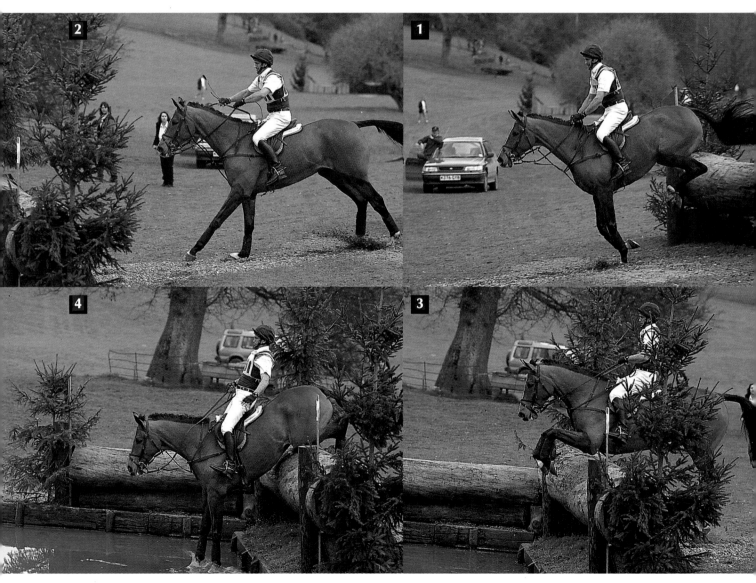

JUMPING OUT OF WATER ON PILOT LIGHT

Coming out of water can be just as difficult as jumping in. Sometimes problems occur because the rider is so relieved at having stayed in one piece jumping into water that he or she loses concentration. It is important to keep an even stride coming through water because that will minimise splashing, which can be blinding. With this fence at Windsor, I applied the same principle as jumping a chevron/arrowhead – keep the horse coming and let him use his natural instinct to tell him when to take off. After jumping this fence well at Windsor in 1992, Pilot Light went on to finish third.

FOOTBRIDGE ON NEW YORK

A fence actually in the water should be approached with some caution to make sure the horse doesn't stumble. New York has come in awkwardly (1), but I've maintained contact with his mouth and kept him moving forwards over this footbridge fence at Ston Easton Horse Trials (2).

CORNER IN WATER ON CARTOON

This big corner in the Trout Hatchery at Burghley in 1995, designed by Mark Phillips, was the first corner ever actually sited in water in this country. Not surprisingly, it caused severe apprehension and much nervous talk among riders. If the alternative hadn't been so difficult, I definitely would have considered it. In the end most horses cleared the corner, if somewhat messily. It had a steep downhill approach to the water, in which you had about two strides before take-off. However, this wasn't a fence where seeing a stride was a priority – an even contact on the horse's mouth and even pressure with the legs was more important. Cartoon isn't the snappiest of jumpers but I have let him jump it on his instinct and so he's been careful and, in fact, a lot neater than many others who took off too far back and had to stretch.

WATER COMPLEX ON STAR ROLE

This was the penultimate fence on the course at Compiègne, a two-star three-day event in France, and it rode quite awkwardly. It came at 9½ minutes and was a lot to ask of a tired horse at this stage, but Star Role still feels like a Ferrari, even though it is only his second three-day event run. I ride him forwards to get plenty of impulsion into the water because it is only one long stride to the bank (2). I leave his head and neck alone so that he can jump freely through the air (3), and I keep my bodyweight back so that I am secure when we land and can push on up the bank (4). Star Role is surprised to find he can only bounce on top of the bank before jumping off but I keep thinking forwards and he jumps neatly off it (5) and takes the one stride to an angled palisade well (6), before galloping to the finish.

SLOPE INTO WATER ON ALL HONOUR

I sit back coming down this steep slope into water at Bicton on All Honour, because although he's inexperienced, he is bold and thinks that downhill means gaining speed (1). I thought he was going too fast for a young horse approaching water and so I hold him firmly and get his head up, although still maintaining leg pressure (2). All Honour jumps confidently into the water (3); I slip the reins and sit back in case he trips over, which he nearly does (5), more due to the drag of the water than to lack of athleticism on his part. His brain is thinking fast, but the water holds him back and I sit still while he regains his balance (6), jumps out positively and is up and running for the next fence (7).

WATER COMPLEX WITH TURTLE

In the photographic sequence above Turtle leaps bravely into the same water complex at Bicton (1). His back legs go under (2), nearly causing him to sit down, but he is an athletic horse and quickly picks himself up to move through the water like a little fish.

This is typical behaviour from a courageous young horse, especially one from New Zealand as they tend to be brave in water. It emphasises the need for a rider to be ready for anything.

JUMPING OUT OF WATER ON SCORPION

The sequence on the right occurred during one of my earlier attempts at Badminton and you can see how much longer my stirrups were in those days! Badminton was a pretty tall order for this horse, and quite soon after this doomed attempt, he was sold as a hunter. We met the bank coming out of the famous Badminton Lake quite neatly (1), but I think he was getting mentally tired; as you can see, something seems to have gone horribly wrong coming out over the hut affair afterwards (2). However, we crawl over it and somehow stay together – I have a principle that if I can still see the horse's ears there is some hope! Scorpion stayed on his feet here, but shortly afterwards I seem to remember that we came to a grinding halt on the course and retired. These pictures show how quickly things can change from being on target to being a complete disaster.

WATER CROSSING WITH HIGHLY RATED

Here at Ston Easton we jump a narrow vertical, bounce down a bank into the river, take one stride across the water, up a bank and bounce to another narrow vertical. If you ride positively into the first element as if you were jumping a large oxer into a showjumping combination, then the rest should go smoothly. If you get an awkward first jump (1), things can go from bad to worse. Highly Rated survives the experience but you can tell by my hand signals (4) that by the time we arrive in the water I feel we need to push on to get the one stride in the water. If I had risked a messy jump out of the water, Highly Rated would probably have tripped and missed the vertical.

WATER CROSSING WITH NEW YORK

The same complex at Ston Easton, viewed from the other side. This was New York's first advanced run (and he was placed). He is more forward-going than Highly Rated and he has a big stride. Here he takes too long a stride into the water, so instead of chasing him across I've got his ears up my nose in an effort to shorten his stride (2) and get a neat jump up. It looks a bit unstylish, but New York jumps the last element neatly (4) and we're turning in the air, looking for the next fence and saving time (5). This sequence demonstrates that at the end of the day there are no style prizes, and getting from A to B is all-important.

NEW YORK AT A WATER COMPLEX

This year the water at Gatcombe had a vertical jump into it, followed about three strides later, for the first time, by a footbridge/table-type fence sited in the water. Again, sit quietly and allow the horse enough freedom of his head on the approach so that he can see what he has to do, yet still giving him the

vibes that he's got to jump it.

New York's legs don't look very tidy over the vertical (1), but if he had made a mistake, he would have had enough freedom of his head to have corrected himself. I continue to sit still, and we then maintain an evenness of stride through the water (3). New York picks up well (4), and as you can see by the way he bounds over the second fence (5), that this is a classy horse. He is only seven and hasn't done very many advanced competitions.

As we jump over the bridge, I keep hold of his head even though there isn't another fence to jump, because we are landing in water (6).

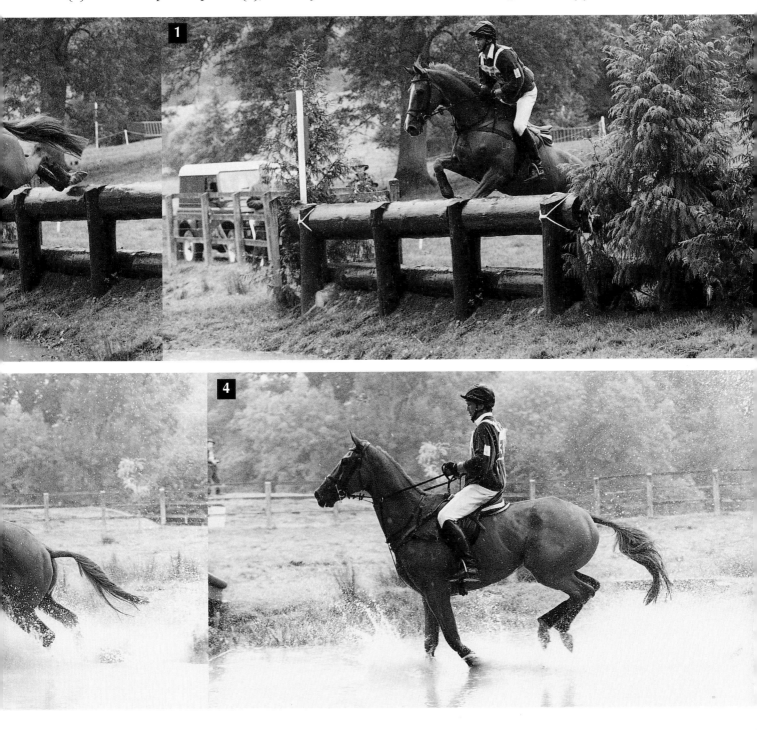

NEW YORK AT A BOUNCE INTO WATER

This beautifully decorated bounce into water at Hartpury was sited opposite the start box, which could tempt a horse's attention to wander, so you needed to ride at it more positively than if it was out in the back of beyond.

A bounce into water should be ridden at more strongly in case the horse is surprised by the water. Even if you see a bad stride coming into the fence, keep moving the horse up to it rather than just sitting and waiting for it to come. It is best to meet the first element with a little too much impulsion than not enough. Even before we've landed over the first, I'm pressing New York into the next element (1), picking up my hands (2) and committing him to get on into the water (3).

BOUNCE INTO WATER ON SCHIROUBLES

This fence into the Badminton Lake in 1990 was not the most brilliant piece of design because the combination of bright white rails, sunlight and water (1) was confusing and there were a couple of crashing falls. It hasn't been seen since. However, Schiroubles was a brave and neat jumper, so I was able to ride him quietly to the first element and give him a chance to sight it and take it all in. If he had been a nervous horse I would have had to have ridden with more pressure and to have risked him not being so tidy with his legs. Schiroubles was a nightmare horse on the flat – he used to buck when warming up and we would score quite appalling marks in the dressage – but he loved the cross-country, as you can see by the verve with which he exits the Lake, as compared with Scorpion's attempt (pages 118–19). Schiroubles went through the water very fast and he must have thought that he had to jump the bank and punt in one, hence the extravagant movement (2). On this occasion he distinguished himself by scoring 81.8 in the dressage – but this was by no means his worst effort!

THE KIDNEY POND WITH NEW YORK

This was a pretty serious water complex at Bramham where the three elements all came up very fast. Horses had to jump over a box-type obstacle into the water (not shown), then over a hanging log with a waterfall and a significant

drop (1) and then make a sharp turn to an angled hanging log. I haven't jumped anything like this since the Los Angeles Olympics where there was a similar obstacle. New York was the first horse on the course that day and the important thing here was to make sure that once we were in the water, we kept going forwards rather than worry about looking for a stride. There was so much spray (2) that I couldn't see much and it was a case of keeping New York going and relying on his natural instinct to jump.

WATER COMPLEX ON STAR ROLE

This element was narrow faced with a big spread, so you needed plenty of power approaching it, which is why it is best not to turn too sharply into it

This final element on the direct route was even narrower, with a wider spread, and it was a big question for a young horse, which is why only a few people took it on their more experienced horses, including the winner of the class

The black arrows indicate the route I took in order to get more of a run at the final element

When I walked the course at Savernake I thought that this double into water would involve a forward-going two strides, but on my first ride of the day, Star Role, who is only seven and not very experienced, I soon realised that this wasn't quite the case. He got two-and-a-half strides, which propelled him very close to the rails into the water and he had to jump them from a standstill. In order to keep him going, I get myself behind the movement and apply firm leg pressure but don't pull on the reins so that Star Role can balance his head. As you can see by the third picture, we have recovered the situation. Star Role never felt as if he would refuse and he dug himself out of trouble after I made a mistake, which is exactly the characteristic one looks for in a good cross-country horse. We both came home a bit wiser and with my later rides I came into this combination somewhat slower and got the required three strides in between.

For the direct route, you need to be committed and on a forward stride when you land in the water. Be aware that as all the horses will be landing in more or less the same place, it can sometimes make the base uneven, causing a horse to peck on landing

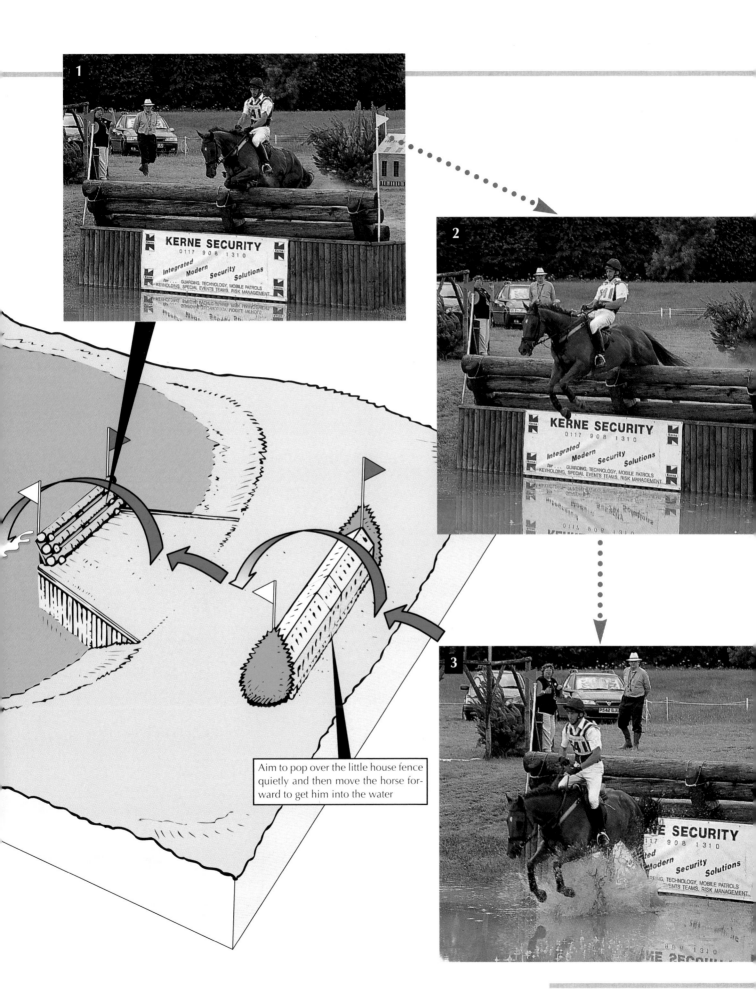

Aim to pop over the little house fence quietly and then move the horse forward to get him into the water

WHAT TO DO AT THE EVENT

Course-walking

When walking a cross-country course it is almost as important that the rider pays as much attention to the ground between the fences as the fences themselves, and that they note the places where it is safe to gallop on. Look out for sloping ground, rough patches and twisting woodland paths. Be prepared for the sort of things that a horse might spook at, such as advertising boards or people walking the course beside narrow woodland paths, or sights that might suddenly faze a horse, such as the general public crowding around a water complex. It is much easier to go fast across country if you know exactly what is coming next.

In woodland, particularly, it is important to remember which corners lead to jumps, and therefore where you shouldn't be going too fast, and which are followed by a clear run where it is safe to motor on. Forested tracks can be hard to ride; they tend not to have much of a view and, as a result, can be dispiriting for both you and the horse. Courses such as Saumur and Compiègne in France and Tweseldown in England can be a bit disheartening because there is no outlook, whereas park courses such as Badminton, Burghley or Windsor are more encouraging because they give you more of a sense of progress.

When entering a one-day event I try and organise it so that I am riding at the same level of cross-country all day, in other words just novice classes or intermediate or advanced, unless I know the course very well. The novice track tends to get less attention than the intermediate which, in turn, gets a quicker look than the advanced. I rarely walk a one-day event course on the day before I am going to ride it; I would rather get up early and walk it on the day so that it is fresh and isn't confused with the previous day's activities.

Novice riders should try, if possible, to walk the course when it's actually being ridden. You can learn a lot from watching other people. Even at novice level you'll see a couple of top riders with their young horses, and just watching the way they approach a fence and maintain their rhythm will help you. Like most riders, I don't worry about measuring the course at a one-day event. It is rare for them to be measured exactly anyway, and I just ride as fast as is sensible and appropriate for the particular horse and course. After all, there is less at stake at a one-day event, which I consider to be part of a horse's preparation for the three-day rather than being the ultimate competition.

At a three-day event I walk the course three times. I like to go on my own at first. This isn't always easy because all the riders will have just been driven around the roads and tracks phases in convoy; but I still try to get away on my own. I find that if I first walk the cross-country course in a group, apprehension can become contagious. On the second and third occasions I am happy to have company, either an experienced rider or one of my pupils if they are also competing. However, I usually stick to my first impression about how I will take a particular fence. It is important to remember that even an experienced rider doesn't necessarily know your horse, so don't feel that you have to follow their advice exactly.

I never walk the course on the actual day of the cross-country at a three-day event, but if I have time and there is a particular fence I want to see jumped, I might look down the startsheet and select a couple of riders to watch.

I also don't like being given too much advice in the ten-minute box. Obviously there are certain snippets of information which I am always grateful to receive, like where the best landings are, where the going has suddenly become deep, or whether the movement of sun and shadow are causing horses to make mistakes. I wouldn't necessarily change my

mind about my chosen route, but it would make me more alert.

Before entering the start-box I always go through the track in my mind and visualise myself jumping round it. I prefer not to watch anyone else riding it because that might confuse my mental image. Sometimes people will tell me afterwards that I didn't look very good over such and such a fence, but it won't stop me doing it the same way on my second horse if I know that that is what will best suit it. Of course it is important to watch other riders and learn from them, but sometimes you have to look objectively at how well they handled the problem fence before you let it influence your final decision.

Making decisions

If I feel worried about a particular complex on the cross-country course and I don't know the horse very well, I am quite happy to consider the alternative 'slower' route if it looks as though it can be negotiated smoothly. I might, of course, change my mind once I've started if the horse gives me a confident feel, although I am always telling my pupils not to change their minds once they have left the start-box! When you're learning it is important to be focused and to make up your mind before you start – although as I have said, it is not always advice that I follow myself!

Sometimes riders get it into their head that they must do a certain direct route even if it is really bothering them, and then they will build up a mental block about it. Personally, I am all for keeping my confidence levels up and I don't think there's anything wrong with opting for the slower route at a fence if I'm worried about it. Some riders will try anything for the hell of it because they have scored a poor dressage mark and are out of the running, but if things aren't going well for me, I usually reason that they're not going to get better!

If you can build up skill in riding smoothly through long routes when necessary, it will pay off on the bigger occasions when it sometimes becomes apparent that a certain complex is causing problems for everyone. This is where the earlier training exercises at home, such as taking verticals at an angle, come into play.

If you are aiming to take the longer route at a fence, always slow the horse down as you approach it and think 'slow but economic'. Don't get in a position where you have approached too fast and have to argue with the horse, because that wastes time: the calmer the horse, the quicker you can go. Make sure you have mapped out the route through the fence in your head so that you can keep looking ahead and maintaining a rhythm, rather than suddenly yanking the horse around because you haven't prepared yourself properly.

There is no need to get into a state about distances and strides at so-called 'bogey' fences. It's easy to start making cross-country riding sound terribly technical when it really is a straightforward thing – there's only two real gears: galloping or coming down a gear before a combination fence!

Some riders don't give their horse enough credit for coping, but if you dominate a horse, it can't use its natural ability. Instead of thinking: 'I've absolutely got to get two strides in here', aim to present the horse at the right speed and let him do what he wants to get over the fence. However, while it's important not to panic and throw the horse at the fence, there *is* a happy medium – so don't just sit there and hope for the best!

The key to success is the strength of the canter before the fence: the horse must have enough power to choose how it best negotiates the fence. If I'm keyed up about a combination fence, I sometimes slap the horse gently on the shoulder as soon as it lands over the first element and take a bit of a hold just to wake up both him and myself.

Finally, when you've cleared a difficult fence, don't sit back and put your feet up. You might feel like celebrating your survival but it doesn't actually mean that it's time for a gin and tonic – there's still the rest of the course to do. We've all made the mistake of relaxing and switching off, and that can lead to a really annoying error.

Top left: This fence was in the middle of the second water complex. It was a big step up onto a bank with a bounce distance to the log pile drop, and I picked up 20 penalties on Jagermeister: he tripped up the step, fell onto his knees and could not jump over the log

Above: The fourth fence: I got the feeling that the course designer didn't want anyone with a 'ditch problem' to get any further!

Top right: Nearing the end of the course a huge filled-in corner to test the riders' accuracy over the boldest most direct route. I'm looking for something to focus on when riding a good straight approach which will save vital seconds

Centre right: Walking through the water at the first water complex to check its depth and footing

Right: This fence looked really wide and some horses even banked it. It had a tricky narrow approach, but at least with a rounded top you had slightly more room for error

Below: The picturesque roads and tracks phase at Windsor

Riding the Roads and Tracks

When you first inspect the two roads and tracks phases, A and C, it is again important to observe the going. Look out for rough, stony places, boggy going, tarmac, or heavy sand, which is what we had to put up with at the World Games in The Hague in 1994. The sand there was very deep, the going was diabolical, and it took a lot out of the horses. Like many riders, I am afraid I find roads and tracks extremely boring, so the mental exercise of covering 4km (2½ miles) per minute does break it up a bit. The aim is to proceed at a normal working trot, but if there is a deep boggy patch, for instance, I might want to walk my horse through that bit, which means that I will need to have cantered on the preceding kilometre in order to make up the time.

Nowadays the roads and tracks phases are very well marked and it's nearly impossible to miss a flag or a checkpoint, but after a somewhat dramatic incident at Burghley where I was erroneously eliminated (and later reinstated) for missing a checkpoint because there happened to be no tick by my name, I make a point of waving, grinning and speaking to officials so they can't forget that I went past!

Use a stopwatch which is clear to read and very simple to use; you don't want to be panicking about what it says when you are halfway around. Ride Phase A with your stirrups at steeplechase length, and aim to finish with two minutes to spare. Those two minutes can be very handy if you have miscalculated where the finish is. If I am riding an excitable horse, I walk him when I'm in sight of the finish, so as not to get him in a frenzy.

Phase C, the second roads and tracks, is longer and comes immediately after the steeplechase. The first minute would probably be spent lowering my stirrup leathers a few holes, checking that all four shoes were on and perhaps having the horse quickly washed down if the weather was hot. Then I would set off walking, perhaps leading the horse, until my watch said four minutes, when I'd hop on and trot, which should get me to a kilometre in six minutes; after that I'd stay trotting and aim to reach each

Below: It is important to start the steeplechase phase at the required speed, as it is difficult to make up time once you've started. The horse should be standing off the fences, so no time is wasted in the air

kilometre point at four-minute intervals. The reason for taking six minutes for the first kilometre is to allow the horse to get his breathing back to normal after the steeplechase.

If you are late starting this phase, perhaps due to a shoeing problem or a tack adjustment, don't feel you have to go flat out early on to catch up the lost time immediately. This is why I don't walk until the end is in sight, in case I have misjudged it. Again, I would aim to finish Phase C with two minutes to spare, which would give me twelve minutes in the official ten-minute box.

Riding the Steeplechase

The steeplechase is the second phase – B – of the four speed and endurance phases at a three-day event, and involves, as the name implies, jumping racing-type fences at a faster speed; in fact at several European three-day events this phase is actually run on a real racecourse. The aim is always to finish within the time allowed – it is a silly place to get time penalties unless the going is deep or you have a particularly slow horse.

The time allowed is always so many metres per minute – for instance, at a two-star level three-day event it is 660 metres per minute. I walk the steeplechase track with a measuring wheel and every time it registers the official speed per minute, I note exactly where that is so that I know where I should be when each minute falls.

I set my stopwatch when the starter tells me I have five seconds to go, because fiddling around setting my watch when they actually say 'go' can waste a couple of seconds (of course, the trick then is to *remember* that I've set it five seconds early!).

The aim is therefore to arrive at my first minute marker on 1.05 minutes, and the theory is that if I stick to that pace and the course has been measured exactly, I'll finish five seconds under the time, which is perfect. What you don't want is a mad rush to make up time over the last few fences, because this is dangerous and a waste of energy, and it makes it more difficult to slow down at the end. Some horses

naturally have a higher cruising speed than others, and if the horse is jumping well, it is probably best to stay at the same speed rather than interfering.

The steeplechase phase is ridden at 100 metres faster per minute than the cross-country phase, and the fences – in England anyway – are made of sloping brush, which is much more forgiving than a solid cross-country fence. This means that you can gently move the horse up to the fences more quickly, rather than slowing him down beforehand, and get him jumping quickly over the fence, rather than hovering in the air. However, the more forgiving and tempting nature of steeplechase fences does not mean that it is an opportunity to go wild and gallop flat out.

Continental steeplechase fences might consist of anything from combinations, to fences with ditches, or stone walls, and sometimes the course runs in a complicated shape, such as a figure of eight. I find that these tracks are good for young horses – they usually jump them well and it provides a useful school before the actual cross-country – but the more diverse and solid nature of these fences means that it is even more important to ride sensibly, and not on a 'wing and a prayer'.

The ten-minute box

At a three-day event there is a compulsory ten-minute halt after Phase C, the second roads and tracks, which takes place in an officially confined space. Its purpose is for the official vets to check the horse's fitness before allowing it to continue on Phase D, the cross-country course, and for horse and rider to be refreshed and made comfortable and therefore in the best possible physical and mental state for the excitements ahead. The ten-minute box is really the hub of cross-country day, and the organisation therein by a rider's team can sometimes make or break a performance. It is the part of the three-day event which probably takes most organisation, and Jayne now describes her crucial role.

'First, I choose a site in the "box", preferably in the shade and near the water supply, and away from loud-speakers, other horses starting and finishing and anyone who might come and wind Andrew up! It can be a nightmare for riders if they get pestered with questions and unnecessary advice, and I always feel sorry for anyone who gets interviewed for television at this stage.

'As the rider and horse come into the box, at a compulsory trot and on a loose rein, the vets will be watching for any signs of injury, fatigue or stress in the horse. The rider dismounts, and only when the vets have given the "all-clear" may an assistant come forward to hold the horse. The vets will take the horse's temperature and check its respiratory and heart rates.

'While this is going on, the assistant has several things to do, all without hindering the vets. I loosen the noseband, always by four holes as I can then remember where it was done up before, and I loosen the girth and put the stirrups to Andrew's cross-country length. I check that the boots haven't slipped and that all four shoes are still intact. If there is a shoe missing or some risen clenches, I get my helper to find the farrier and bring him over to our "camp" with a spare shoe.

'By this time the vets should have finished. Andrew and I like to hear the results of the temperature and heart-rate tests – I would hope to to see our horses with a heart rate in the seventies or eighties. Sometimes a young or excitable

horse will have a higher rate than others, which may be checked again after five minutes to ensure that it has come down. This should come down on subsequent occasions as the horse gains more experience of the pattern of the three-day event.

'We then return to our site with the horse, and while I and another helper set to work on him, Andrew is packed off to the loo. (This may sound obvious, but it is no good leaving the loo visit until the last minute!) Some riders seem to have a crowd of helpers, but we find two is enough.

'The horse is washed down around the neck, legs and sweating areas. If it is very cold we take care not to wet the loins or back muscles excessively as this can lead to chilling and muscle cramps. If it is very hot weather we will use iced water, but the important thing is for the water to be scraped off immediately. We might then put a rug on the horse's back to keep the muscles warm.

'If the bridle needs changing, do this straightaway as it should be tied on with a shoelace threaded through the first plait – this prevents the

rider pulling the bridle off if they fall over the horse's head – and it can take time.

'We like to remove the horse's brushing boots – we use "Style" boots which have strong Velcro and are light and quick and easy to use – to check the horse's legs for cuts. We wipe the inside of the boots to remove any mud or grit which could cause rubbing, then towel dry them and put them back on. The studs are also checked at this stage. When working in a pair, it is a good idea for one person to take the boots off and wipe the legs and boots and for the other to dry the boots and put them back on. The same person should put on all four boots, so that each leg receives an even pressure.

'I give the horse a drink and am quite happy if it drinks up to half a bucket of water. If it doesn't want to drink, I will squeeze a sponge out in its mouth. It should then be led around to prevent any stiffness.

'The rider should also be offered a drink. Andrew will only have still water, but some people like sports drinks with electrolytes. Fizzy drinks are not recommended! Most riders don't want to eat at this stage, but if there is a hold on the course you can be waiting a long time. It is entirely a personal thing – some riders like chocolate biscuits, some

We always encourage our horses to drink at events, so that they get used to drinking in the ten-minute box

have glucose sweets, others resort to a cigarette. I have even seen a rider tuck into a huge French stick filled with salad! It is always a good idea to keep sandwiches and drink in the kit because even if the rider doesn't want it then, they will when they finish.

'It depends on the rider's temperament as to how much information you give them about what has been happening on the course. Some people like to be psyched up and to hear about the falls and dramas, but generally, the golden rule is to instil confidence and at the same time make them aware of the fences which are causing problems. Believe me, this is a very fine line! It is important to leave the rider alone while they go through the course in their mind, and to have a programme available for them to recall their minute markers. If also helps if you are aware of the markers yourself. I lay out a dry sweatshirt and gloves for Andrew in case he wants them, but I try not to bother him with unnecessary questions, and I advise others to do the same!

'At the five-minute stage, the horse is offered another drink. The noseband is done up, the saddle repositioned and the girth tightened. Once the tack has been adjusted, apply grease, ideally wearing a glove, down the front of all four legs and behind the knees and around the heels. The stifle and knee areas are the most vulnerable, so make sure that they are well covered. Don't apply grease high up the horse's chest because this can hinder its sweating. Take care when doing all this, because some horses know what is coming and get excited. Getting kicked is not helpful to either you or the rider!

'Remove your grease glove – getting grease on the reins or saddle will not be popular either – and turn your attention to the rider, who should be ready and waiting. Once they are aboard, be ready to make tack adjustments, or towel dry anything that is still wet.

'At three minutes, check the rider has set his watch to zero and send them off to trot and canter around to get the horse back in tune. This is best done out by the start and away from the hordes of

people and equipment which inevitably fill up the box. The helper should somehow manage to stay nearby, but without getting in the way! The girth should be checked – we use short elastic girths on a flapless Butet cross-country saddle, mainly because they are much quicker and easier to tighten and this system doesn't require a surcingle, again saving precious seconds.

'Meanwhile, helper number two is filling buckets ready for the finish and tidying up.

'Down at the start I watch Andrew take a few deep breaths and focus his mind. I like to be nearby because a lot of horses get wound up, and occasionally one even tries to jump out of the start-box, which is pretty disconcerting for the rider. Just having someone standing there can help to keep a horse calmer. Sometimes I hold out a handful of

grass as enticement – but don't let the horse eat it! The main aim is for both rider and horse to have an unflustered start.

'Everyone involved will then be willing them to have a successful round. I have a love-hate relationship with the closed-circuit monitor which is usually available for connections to watch in the ten-minute box: I love to watch Andrew going well, but I feel anguished at every stumble or hairy moment, and despair at a refusal or, worse still, a fall. I am also constantly aware of the horse and how it looks. Is it tired? Did it hit its knee or stifle somewhere? I start thinking ahead about any bruising that may require attention later.

'As the horse returns, the rider will dismount and take off the saddle to weigh in, while the vets check the horse's heart and respiratory rate and take

its temperature. My mothering instinct then comes to the fore and I like to take the horse, because I think it should be with a person that knows it. I also like to see the results of the vets' tests, although I can see the respiratory rate for myself! Before any congratulations, commiserations or post-mortems are carried out, the horse must be cared for: those first minutes are very important, and if it is hot weather it can be critical. As you walk the horse back from the weigh-in to your personal site, undo the shoelace around the bridle. Remove the bridle and give the horse a drink of water at normal temperature. Again, I don't mind if he drinks half a bucket – if I'm hot and thirsty, this is what I would want to do, and his body needs to re-hydrate quickly to replace the fluids lost by exertion and sweating.

'We remove all the horse's gear, which should take moments. However, if he was bandaged I would start washing him off before removing these, because at this stage the most important thing is to cool his body temperature. Again, work in a pair with one person washing and the other quickly scraping off the excess water. Go around the horse's body two or three times if necessary, and use iced water if conditions require it. At the Atlanta Olympics the horses stood in an area of demisting fans, which proved very effective.

'Only when the horse is washed and being walked around do you start listening to how it went out there on the course...'

Warming up and starting

At a three-day event, the horse has obviously done a fair bit before it starts on the cross-country and so the warm-up is just a couple of minutes walking and trotting. At a one-day event it is important to assess the difficulty of the first couple of fences on the cross-country course. Do they require accuracy, or are they just nice straightforward fences which allow your horse to get into a rhythm? If I felt that my horse needed to be a bit sharp for the first few fences, I would warm him up a little more than usual, but if the early part of the course was fairly straightforward, the warm-up would be more laid back.

When it is getting near starting time, go to the start and find out how many horses are due to go before you. I usually start warming up when there are about two or three before me. I canter around and hop over the practice fence three or four times, keeping the horse moving. Don't start warming up too early because if you keep stopping and starting you will switch your horse off.

If I am riding a horse which lacks confidence, I spend less time warming it up, aiming to 'rev it up' quickly at the last moment so that it doesn't have too much time to worry about what's going on.

A strong horse would get no warm-up at all, not even a canter – with Jagermeister I just set off cold! I also find that some of the novice horses which have come out of racing don't need much warm-up either. Also, too much warming up can have a negative effect on a horse which tends towards a chicken nature, as I mentioned above.

A nappy horse needs to be kept on the move, and I make sure that someone warns me when there are thirty seconds to go so that we don't have to stand still.

If a horse is very excitable, it is helpful to have a helper around to tease it a little with a handful of grass. This should persuade it to stand still and think about something else.

As a horse progresses through the grades it should become quieter at the start, psyching itself up calmly. However, remember that a horse which has been allowed to get wild may not always think what it is doing, and if it gets too revved up it can't breathe properly, which won't help its stamina.

Riding to time

Firstly it is important to remember that the time set for a cross-country phase at a three-day event is

achievable – that's why it's there, to make the competition more interesting – unless the conditions on the day are extreme, that is very hot or very wet. If your horse is fit and jumps cleanly, and you have absorbed the lie of the course properly and know where you can let the handbrake off, you should have a chance. Measure the course with a wheel, and as with the steeplechase, memorise where the minute markers come. If the course measures longer or shorter than it should, which sometimes happens, you will have to adjust your markers accordingly.

This may sound obvious, but it is crucial that the landmarks you choose for minute markers will be there on the day. An ice-cream van, which is liable

to move, is obviously not a good idea! However, trees, loos, loudspeakers, public crossing points and, obviously, fences are more useful. I write these down, usually during my second course-walk, and memorise them on the third walk. I also write them into the map in the programme.

I don't go in for writing a lot of instructions on my arm before setting off, usually just the speeds for Phases A and C, as I prefer to keep it simple. I

can usually remember the steeplechase time, and I try to memorise my minute markers on the cross-country course. [The speeds required are 520mpm, 550mpm, 570mpm at one, two and three/four-star level respectively.] Most people's gallop work at home is done with a stopwatch, and with practice you will know instinctively how fast you have to go in order to achieve a certain stretch of gallop within a certain time.

Again, I set my stopwatch five seconds early, and I look at it regularly at the beginning of the course in order to establish the right pace. In an ideal situation I hope to reach the three-minute marker on time because then I know I have found the right speed and all I have to do is to keep up that momentum. There is no point in setting off like a lunatic and getting half a minute up on the clock, because if you try and slow down after that you will lose your rhythm. Conversely, there is no cause for alarm if you find yourself ten seconds down at the three-minute marker, because if the horse has a good engine you can increase its 'turbo'. Always try to ride quietly, and be economic with your own movements;

busy flapping reins and legs will not help your horse.

You also need to allow for terrain. At Windsor, for instance, there is a steep two-minute climb at the start of the course where you are bound to get a bit behind, but the rest of the course is fast and flat and you can make it up. On the other hand, some courses are twisty at the end, and in those situations you need to be a little up on the time. This is why attention to detail on course-walking is so important; when riding, you must be constantly looking and thinking ahead, not just at the fence you are jumping but at the next one and at the ground in between. If you just live for the moment, you will waste time constantly manoeuvring the horse back on track.

Sometimes you have to accept that you are simply not going to make the time. Not every horse is built for speed, and there may be mitigating circumstances, such as when riding a very strong, pulling horse. It is better then to accept the facts of a few time penalties and jump the jumps properly, rather than chasing the time and tipping over.

The tactics of time-keeping may seem daunting at first, and are a great deal to take in for an inexperienced rider; but it's surprising how easily you get used to it. It's then that maintaining concentration can be a problem – too much satisfaction at one's brilliance on being up on the time is extremely dangerous, and certainly my pleasant dreams of how I'm going to spend the prize money have been rudely interrupted by disaster on more than one occasion!

Finishing

If the horse feels tired as you approach the end of the course, don't throw it at the fences: keep hold of its head, keep a shorter rein, and above all, sit still. If you flap about you will unbalance it. Then you can ask yourself why it was tired, because it shouldn't be. There is no excuse for a really tired horse, and if it gets in that state, then it shouldn't have been there.

Don't be in a hurry to stop suddenly just because you're glad to get home. Jerking a horse to a stop or wheeling it around abruptly doesn't look attractive, and you can lame it that way. When walking the course, check how much room there is to pull up, because some events don't plan for this. You don't want to hit a car, trip over a rope or ride over someone's picnic! At a one-day event, unless it is an advanced class when I would have to weigh in, I often trot back to the lorry. People might think this a bit hard on the horse, but an intermediate or a novice hasn't exactly run the marathon, and keeping it moving will all help with its fitness and muscle tone.

As you get off the horse, look quickly for cuts and minor injuries. In hot weather it is important to wash him off immediately; the water should be scraped off straightaway and then he should be kept walking for ten to fifteen minutes until his breathing is back to normal. Never, ever smother him with towels, as this will trap the heat around his body and prevent him cooling.

After a three-day event run, the horse should be walked around for about forty-five minutes and he may need more than one washing off; *don't* just shove him back in the stable. Depending on the going on the course, or the type of horse, you might want to stand his legs in iced water or whirly or jacuzzi boots, which should come up to his knees; but it is worth remembering that you may need official permission to use some types of ice boot. We then bandage the horse's legs, normally with fibregee underneath, and let him have half an hour's grazing before taking him back to the stable and feeding him.

The horse should then be left in peace for about three hours, after which we take him out and trot him up, preferably on a hard, flat surface. If I am worried about him having bruised himself, I might apply a clay compound to soothe bruising and if a shoe has been lost this can also be applied to the sole of the foot. If our horse is sound and healthy, then we just tidy his rugs and bandages, pet him and say good night.

Never, ever be tempted to walk your horse around all night or to use machines in a desperate attempt to make him sound in time for the following morning's veterinary inspection. If you need to do this, you shouldn't even be thinking of showjumping. In any case, sometimes a good night's rest is all that is needed.

If there is a problem with your horse's soundness, be careful how you treat it. Many seemingly innocuous ointments and powders contain forbidden substances which will show up in a routine dope test the next day. If in doubt, consult the British Horse Trials Association's rule book. The days of administering a sachet of 'bute into the evening feed are long gone, and if you use it, you stand to be fined or banned. In the old days, many riders relied heavily on the use of 'bute to get horses through the trot-up. Nowadays, however, there is no substitute for preparing a horse correctly, and the three-day event really starts at the point when you leave home with a sound, fit horse.

HORSE MANAGEMENT

Feeding for fitness

with Jayne Nicholson

Although I have a basic feeding plan for the whole yard, each horse is fed independently, according to its size, type and character – we have a long-standing joke that when a horse is going well, it's because it's being well ridden, but when it's going badly it's because it's not being fed properly! When a horse arrives in the yard, the first thing we have to decide is whether it will hold its weight or 'run up light', whether it is a type which will need revving up or calming down, and at what level it will be competing. If it is the sort of horse which holds its condition and perhaps tends to be lazy, it would be fed an oat-based diet. Cartoon comes into this category – he is a good doer and a laid-back character so I feed him more heating food but with a controlled hay ration. A horse which doesn't hold its condition and tends to be nervy would be fed more nuts, barley and carbohydrates. Dawdle is this sort, a hyped-up, nervous horse on whom it is hard to keep weight, so he would receive more fattening, non-heating feed and more hay.

At the end of the season the horses are roughed off and turned out. They do not receive any concentrate feed, just hay and grass, because we

Micronised barley

Lightly crushed oats

Mollichaff

Glucose powder

POWDERED GLUCOSE

Lump rock salt

Country event cubes

Equilibra feed balancer

Sugarbeet pellets

Country mix (coarse mix)

Essentials elements of Jayne's feeding programme

like their systems to have a good clean-out; it also means that they will be keen to eat hard food when they come in. They are turned out without rugs or shoes and in bunches of eight to ten, so they keep themselves quite fit; thus when they come in again to start work they are still reasonably hard, although quite round in shape. When they come into work, they all have a double dose of wormer and a teeth check. If I was particularly worried about a horse's condition I might consider having it blood-tested, but we are not great fans of this procedure.

To begin with, we feed them a light diet consisting of 75 per cent hay and forage and 25 per cent concentrates. We always use a guaranteed feed because it is free from contamination by forbidden substances which would show up in a routine dope test at a three-day event; this is on the principle that if a feed passes Jockey Club rules, then it should be all right for eventing.

We buy our hay locally, either from a farmer or from a reputable seller. We feed a softish meadow hay in winter and then move on to a harder type in the eventing season. We choose hay more by the smell, which should be sweet, rather than looking for hard rye-grass hay, as Thoroughbreds can be picky about the texture. We feed it in bins rather than haynets which tend to break and are time-consuming to fill.

Most of our horses are bedded on straw, which is still the cheapest bedding and, I think, the most comfortable and cosy for a horse, except for the advanced horses and those doing three-day events or the fatter horse which likes to eat its bedding – these would be kept on paper (Diceabed) bedding. We always keep a few stables aside for paper bedding rather than clearing out ones which have had straw in as this seems to be a more cost-effective method. We also try to stable those horses which are going to travel together, next to each other so that they can make friends – this is particularly good for the youngsters. We try and group fussy feeders together and feed them last, which soon makes them more enthusiastic about their feed!

Feeding according to work

At the start

On starting work, a horse like Buckley Province, who is small and lightly built, would be fed hay ad lib, probably about 22lb (10kg) a day, which is what we would give any horse on whom it is hard to put any weight; for his morning feed he would have 4lb (1.8kg) of a 12 per cent protein nut (we use Hunter Event Cubes); and for his evening feed 4lb nuts, 2lb (0.9kg) micronised flaked barley [which is cooked with infra-red rays, destroying toxins and making it more digestible], half a scoop of Mollichaff [a complementary compound feed which is 6.5 per cent protein and is a blend of straw and molasses], 4lb soaked sugarbeet, plus cod liver oil and an excellent feed balancer called Equilibra, which has been passed by the Jockey Club. Equilibra, which promotes specific bacteria within the gut, thus aiding digestion, is also high in biotin, which enhances hoof growth, and we introduce it slowly, building up to measurements of 500g, depending on the size of the horse.

All the horses also have a lump of natural rock salt in their mangers; they lick it regularly and it encourages the fussy eaters to go to their mangers.

A bigger horse, or one such as Dawdle who isn't a particularly good doer, would be fed 5lb (2.3kg) nuts morning and evening instead of 4lb. If a horse hasn't done all that well over the winter, we would probably start him off with some coarse mix, a complementary feed which is 12 per cent protein.

One month later

After the horses have been in work for about a month and are starting cantering and jumping, they go on to a diet of 50 per cent hay and 50 per cent concentrates. We also turn them out separately for 20-minute periods each day to pick at the spring grass and have a run.

The amount of nuts fed would rise to 5lb (2.3kg)

in both the morning and evening feeds, and if a horse is holding his weight well, I would increase the amount of barley in the evening feed to 3lb (1.3kg). The maximum amount of barley fed would not rise above 4lb (1.8kg). If a horse starts to tend towards being overweight, I would give him oats instead of nuts, or perhaps a combination of the two.

Salt is introduced into the diet for the horses which are working hardest, plus a handful of glucose, that is, an electrolyte mixture. We feel that it is better to introduce the electrolyte mixture gradually and get the horse used to eating it, rather than just giving it to him for the first time at a three-day event and finding that he won't eat it at a time when he needs it most.

When the season starts

As competition starts, the hayload comes down, depending on the type of horse. However, a little horse or a fussy eater would still stay on unlimited amounts of hay. A fatter horse or one that tends towards stuffiness in the wind, would move down to 12lb (5.4kg) hay, given in two loads of 6lb (2.7kg). We soak the hay for the advanced horses for at least 15 minutes to kill the spores.

Before a three-day event

We don't like our horses to be too fat at three-day events because we would prefer them to look the same on the third day as when they started, rather than changing shape drastically; a horse which is carrying excess condition is putting extra weight on his legs and wear and tear on his body.

Before a three-day event, the diet ratio moves to 25 per cent hay, and 75 per cent hard feed. I start feeding more oats, depending on a horse's temperament, and sometimes use racehorse cubes which are 14 per cent protein as opposed to 12 per cent; this helps with the cross-country stamina, but not with the dressage! I would give a three-quarter-bred horse doing a four-star three-day event such as Badminton or Burghley, racehorse cubes to give him all the help I could.

Therefore the average horse would be receiving for his morning feed: 5lb (2.3kg) nuts, 2lb (0.9kg) oats; for his evening feed: 5lb nuts, 2lb barley, 2lb oats, one-third of a scoop of chaff, 2lb sugar beet. A skinnier horse would get half a scoop of chaff and 3lb (1.3kg) sugar beet; the sugar content in beet boosts a horse's energy levels and keeps him interested in his feed.

All the horses continue to have electrolytes and cod liver oil, while I keep an eye on the looseness of the droppings – too firm droppings is a sign of dehydration.

A point to remember with a small-framed horse is that you don't want to overface him; I prefer a horse to finish his feed completely, rather than pick at it and leave some.

Fit for the job
At the start of the season

When our horses come in from their winter rest, they start work on the horse-walker, which can take five horses at a time. It is 18m (60ft) wide inside and the horses walk on a wet sand base. They start by doing half an hour, working up to an hour in the second week. They might also go on a treadmill for a short time, particularly if they haven't been on it before, while they are still unshod; it gets them used to the noise of the machine. We also believe that this is a better introduction to work than just getting straight on an unfit horse's back, coupled with the fact that we have a lot of horses to work in a limited amount of daylight.

In the third week we start schooling in the outdoor arena, giving each horse 20 minutes work, followed by 30 minutes on the horse-walker. We usually clip them in that week as well, preferring to clip them right out, apart from the legs. We find that trace-clipping is too time-consuming and, anyway, they get sweaty and uncomfortable. Also, if they have come in suffering from rainscald they will feel better with the grease clipped out of the coat, and so will be less susceptible to saddle sores.

After six weeks

In the sixth week, which is generally in mid-February, we start jumping the horses and riding them uphill – we have a hill ride nearby – so that they have a rotated exercise programme of dressage, hillwork and jumping with gridwork. The hill ride is a round trip of about three miles (4.8km), and takes 50 minutes. We trot to the hill, which is very steep, and trot up it twice, which takes about 2 minutes, walking back downhill each time. We build up to doing this five times in one ride. The horses go out in a pair – we hardly ever send any one horse out by itself. A lot of our horses are ex-racehorses and are used to going out in a string. We stick to one ride, which may sound monotonous, but the horses are happy with it and then we know exactly how much work they've done.

If the ground is frozen, then they will go on a treadmill for about 20 minutes, which is quite vigorous exercise, and then have half an hour's walking afterwards or 30 minutes trotting and 30 minutes walking.

We don't gallop the novice horses much; most of them are Thoroughbred and have raced, and we find that we can get them fit enough with working at home. They will do about 35 minutes of dressage each, being worked quite hard, and then have a session on the horse-walker, followed by 20 minutes turned out in the field for a pick of grass and a roll, depending on the weather. We turn them out, wearing boots, individually in small fields so they don't gallop about and injure themselves.

The novices will also have been doing jumping and will have had one or more cross-country schooling sessions before their first event. At this stage the bunch of four-year-olds which have come from the winter sales will get turned out. By this time we like them to have had at least one cross-country schooling session, going confidently around all types of fence.

The intermediate and advanced horses have two gallop sessions before their first event, which would be up a nearby hill, galloping up it and trotting down. A fatter intermediate horse would be galloped twice a week for two weeks in order to achieve a more streamlined figure. We gallop quite fast, not sloppily, doing three sessions of 45 seconds. The trotting back in between helps their recovery, as it does at a three-day event, and teaches them to relax and breathe properly.

On their return to the yard we hose them off, offer them a drink so that they become accustomed to drinking after the fast work at a three-day event, and put them on the horse-walker for 15 minutes to dry off; we then turn them out in the field for a roll and a pick of grass.

During the season

During the competition season, the advanced horses working up to a three-day event have two hillwork sessions a week, plus one gallop. We also gallop them on one of two local all-weather gallops belonging to racehorse trainer Ron Hodges. We gallop at a speed of 700m (760 yards) per minute for 1,400m (1,550 yards), then trot for 2 minutes. This is repeated two or three times.

Three weeks before a three-day event, a three or four-star horse would do a short gallop, either three times uphill or twice around the round 10-furlong gallop, a maximum of twice a week.

On the other days they would have an afternoon session on the treadmill working up to 20 minutes, followed by 15 minutes on the horse-walker, or they would do 15 minutes trotting and 15 minutes walking. The older horses seem to know that a three-day event is approaching and they enjoy their work in the afternoons.

On arrival at a three-day event we might give a horse a short sprint, but usually it will have done its last piece of fast work on the Monday before the event, when any potential injury or shoeing problems should show up.

After the three-day event is over, the horses go back on the walker each day for 45 minutes because they're used to routine and to working. If they have a laid-back character, they might have two hours in the field first and then go on the walker, whereas if they are the hyped up type, they would walk first to calm down before being turned out. Our horses are never doing nothing, unless they are roughed off.

I quite understand that many people would not be able to justify the expense of a horse-walker and/or treadmill, but for a large busy yard like ours these are a necessity and have become a vital part of our training methods with the increasing number of horses that we have collected over the years.

Bits and pieces

Try not to overload your horse with too many gadgets. He should be as free and light as possible. All my horses start off by wearing an ordinary eggbutt snaffle or a French link snaffle, although if a young horse starts to get a bit keen and strong, I don't hesitate to put him into something stronger, usually a vulcanite pelham with the curb chain done up loosely. I ride a lot of novices in pelhams because it gives me more control and helps them to establish a way of going at a more even speed. A vulcanite pelham enables you to slow a horse down subtly, and the more subtle you can be at slowing him down before a fence, the quicker you can go around the course. It works on the nose and jaw, pulling the horse in.

I would rather teach a horse his job at an early stage, than battle along with him leaning and pulling on the snaffle; this will not help with his balance, and you will end up pulling on his mouth over fences. I like to be in a position where I can safely leave a horse alone in between fences, because if you are constantly hauling on his mouth and trying to alter his head position, then you will turn something that is meant to be fun for him into hard work. I sometimes use a gag on a horse which is heavy and leans on the hand, but this is too strong a bit for a young horse. I use an American sweet-iron bit for Jagermeister, who is a desperate puller, and I sometimes school horses at home in a double bridle, although it is too much of a handful to use in competition.

Another favourite bit is the rolled copperwire W-shaped snaffle. This works more on the mouth and is very useful for strong novice horses which have done two or three events and think they know it all. Rather than pulling hard on their mouths, you can just squeeze the reins and they will slow down. I use it to go across country on New York, and I used to use it on the steeplechase with Dawdle to prevent him getting too keen, though he is now back in a

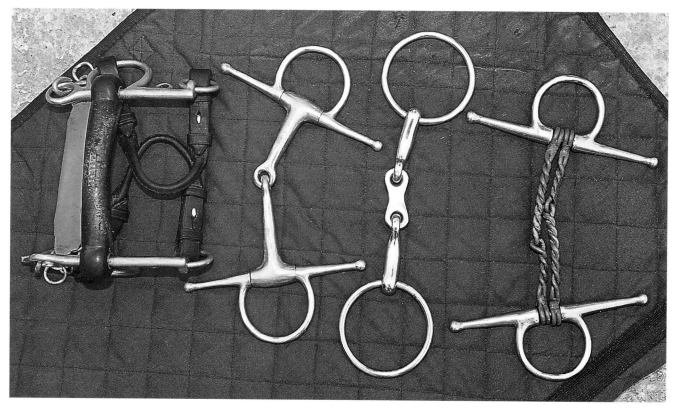

Andrew's choice of bits: *(l to r)* vulcanite pelham with rubber curb guard; Fulmer snaffle; loose-ring French link snaffle; rolled copper W-bit

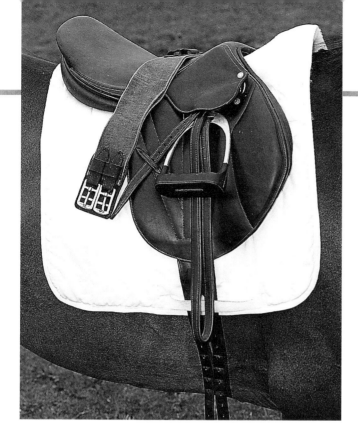

A French Butet cross-country saddle, which provides a closer contact with the horse

snaffle. Often you can return a horse to a snaffle after a couple of outings in a stronger bit; the important thing is not to let him give you a persistently disobedient ride.

All our horses wear running martingales because these give me smoother control for turning, and I always use rubber reins for extra grip. The noseband is usually a cavesson, sometimes with a flash on the bottom; Jagermeister has a rope noseband, which exerts a bit more pressure.

I prefer a lighter type of saddle and use a brand called the Butet, which has just one flap, not much padding in the knee role and a flat seat. It provides a closer contact with the horse and is also helpful in reducing the amount of weight I am carrying. I use an elasticated breastgirth and girths, so the horse can expand comfortably, plus a numnah, depending on the shape of the horse. My stirrups are lightweight and have a wide rubber tread. I am a great believer in putting my feet securely in the stirrups, rather than having them just under my toes as one tends to get taught as a child.

I usually ride the steeplechase with my leathers two holes shorter than at cross-country length, unless I am on a very big horse, in which case I don't ride so short. Leathers which are too short or too long look awful and you end up balancing by

hauling on the horse's mouth. Ride at the length you feel comfortable at and where you can balance without hanging on to the mouth, and you'll have a much better chance of staying on and balancing the horse.

I rarely use over-reach boots on horses, except on the occasional novice, which jumps extravagantly, because I find that they tend to turn over and are useless in water. We use Style boots which are light and quick and easy to put on and don't hold water.

We use different types of stud according to the going, but I try to have just one on the outside of the shoe. Generally I use two small studs on either side of the shoe in hard, slippery conditions or in very deep going, and one large square one in good to soft going. When the going is either very sticky or sandy I don't use any at all, but the horses are all shod with holes in the shoes just in case. I never use them at home for schooling because the horse shouldn't learn to rely on them.

A variety of stud sizes

Andrew and Walk on Top equipped for cross-country

Crash-hat of a standard acceptable to BHTA rules

Knot in end reins – to make the reins a little shorter to enable you to 'slip' them and 'recover' them more easily if the situation requires ie a 'drop' or 'into-space' fence

Unplaited mane in case you need to hold onto something in a tricky moment

I prefer fingerless gloves for a better grip on the rein

Rubber-grip leather reins with two martingale stops

Elastic breast girth to prevent saddle slipping back (even if it is not needed it is a good safety measure)

We prefer to use 'Style' boots for cross country which are protective, light and do not hold water. Easy to put on with strong Velcro straps

With most horses I would not use over-reach boots because they tend to turn over

Treating cross-country injuries

Back protector

Stopwatch: easy to use and with visible display

If your horse is fit and hard before it goes to a competition you will have much more chance of it staying in one piece. However, there are always minor injuries which can occur. For instance, if the horse cuts itself, wash it thoroughly straight away, ensuring there is no grit trapped in the cut which might cause an infection. We use Sudocrem ointment (which is really for humans) or purple spray because these do not have any forbidden substances in them. If the cut is on the leg and can be bandaged, that will help prevent swelling.

Consult the BHTA rule book and always be aware of substances which are forbidden and which might be contained in even an innocuous-looking ointment, because if your horse is subsequently routinely dope-tested at an event and anything shows up in his system, you can be either fined or banned. In the case of a big knee, we might use Ice-tight and/or Animalintex held on with a tubigrip.

A horse which loses a shoe would have Ice-tight applied to the foot, and it would then be parcelled up with sticky black adhesive tape to keep the hoof together until the blacksmith arrives.

If your horse has been prepared properly, it shouldn't tie up (get azoturia); however, sometimes a horse that has had a change of feed or has not been working very hard and then has a more extensive and harder work load can tie up due to the build up lactic acid. Do not feed them protein for a few days and give them Epsom salts in their feed. We encourage our horses to get used to drinking after work because this will help prevent dehydration, which is a major cause of azoturia.

If a horse suffers even a slight tendon strain, it is wrapped up and rested. We apply ice inside a tubigrip and give it an anti-inflammatory drug to reduce the swelling. A horse with a tendon strain always has a holiday. I am lucky in that, having so many horses to ride, I am not tempted to ride too soon one which has suffered a tendon injury. This type of injury, however mild, is a problem that tends to keep coming back – sometimes forever – if care is not taken.

Jayne's first-aid kit for events contains gamgee, Animalintex, Melonin antiseptic pads, Sudocrem, iodine, Elastoplast, tubigrip, cotton wool, a syringe to flush out puncture wounds, witch-hazel, arnica and other homoeopathic ointments.

Conclusion

When I started riding I did a bit of everything, from apple-bobbing to showjumping, but as I gained more experience in my teens it became obvious that the activity which excited me most was cross-country riding. I loved the feeling of being out there on my own with the horse, and the more I did, the greater the buzz.

I also love the fact that the three-day event demands the ultimate in horsemanship. I soon realised that just getting round the cross-country clear was far from being the end of it all. You had to complete in such a way that your horse would be capable of trotting up sound next morning and clearing a round of showjumps. Although the cross-country phase is the highlight, I have learnt that you can't dismiss the other phases, because it is only through attention to the dressage and showjumping skills that a rider gains the ammunition to go well across country. The sport has become so competitive that just flying bravely around the cross-country isn't enough.

Sometimes my working pupils come through the finish on a terrific high, especially if they have completed within the time, and I let them enjoy it for a brief time before I ask them to think back over it. Was there anything they could have done better? I go through my own rounds in my mind straightaway – not a few days later – and think about where I could have improved, and why certain fences might have been negotiated a bit messily. Winning prizes is great, but I believe in leaving the excitement to the owners and to the press, because it's important to me to keep things in perspective. The nature of the sport means that the higher you get, the farther you've got to fall.

If I had to sum up one piece of advice to give anyone wanting to start eventing, it would be to keep your eye in. The most difficult aspect of the sport for the one-horse rider is how to get enough practice to be competitive. A rider should try to jump something almost every day, no matter how small and simple. Although professional riders might only jump their top horse once a fortnight, they will still be jumping regularly. It is very important to me to keep my eye in, to maintain my feel for jumping and to feel confident about it. I ride about twelve horses daily, and hardly a day goes past when I don't jump something.

People probably think that my greatest buzz comes from riding around the top international competitions, but I can get just as excited about a promising novice who goes well at a small event. I more or less know what to expect with my experienced horses, but competing for the first time on a novice horse that goes well can give me a fantastic thrill – I find it immensely satisfying to realise the growing confidence and natural ability of a young horse that I've personally chosen and trained.

Obviously when I'm riding half a dozen horses around the same course in one day I don't expect to feel thrilled every time, and when things *don't* go well it can seem depressing, frustrating and hard work – but I still love it, and could happily ride a dozen more!

Index

Page numbers in *italic* indicate illustrations

INDEX